THE
CRUISE SHIP

A VERY BRITISH INSTITUTION

THE
CRUISE SHIP
A VERY BRITISH INSTITUTION

NICK ROBINS

The History Press

First published 2008

The History Press
Cirencester Road, Chalford,
Stroud, Gloucestershire, GL6 8PE
www.thehistorypress.co.uk

British Library Cataloguing in Publication Data.
A catalogue record for this book is available from the British Library.

ISBN 978 0 7524 4632 5

Printed in Great Britain by Ashford Colour Press Ltd., Gosport, Hants.

CONTENTS

PREFACE

The nineteenth-century romantic vision of the Western Isles of Scotland was responsible for promoting the all-time favourite ten-day cruise round the islands which began in earnest in the 1870s. P&O had offered earlier cruise opportunities, but these were interrupted by the Crimean War. By the 1880s, the Norwegian fjords had become a popular venue and it was not long before cruises to the Mediterranean also became popular. The leading companies in the early days were the Scottish ferry companies; the Edinburgh-based North Company and Salvesen, and on the west coast David MacBrayne Limited, Orme Bros and John MacCallum.

Although the Scots invented the cruise ship they were soon overtaken by a multitude of English companies wanting to reap the benefits of off-season employment for their liners. By the 1900s the yachting cruise had established itself as part of the high society calendar, although there were also attempts to provide cruise travel opportunities at budget prices for the less well-off. Developed through the 1920s, it was the Great Depression that brought cruising to the cheaper mass market and opened the doors of the cruise ship to all comers. Today the cruise industry is dominated by large international groups, of which the P&O and Cunard brands are now American owned, with some of the P&O ships now registered outside Britain in order to attract tax concessions.

The old venue, the Western Isles (including occasional calls at St Kilda), remains very popular with cruise ships large and small. Dedicated smaller vessels are the *Hebridean Princess*, which caters for the top end of the market, and the little *Lord of the Glens.*

The cruise ship continues to grow in size to cater for a new breed of mass tourism. Talk is now of a 500,000 tonner, although the 100,000-ton liners of the Princess Cruises brand and Cunard's new *Queen Mary* would appear to be an optimum size.

This book tells the story from the small beginnings of the nineteenth century to the great industry of the twenty-first century. The story highlights the bigger picture and the historical context of the various developments that unfold towards the present day. Nowadays, however, a declining number of cruise ships can afford to fly the Red or Blue Ensigns.

As always with a book of this kind, the author has received a great deal of help. The text has benefited immensely from critical review by Donald Meek and Richard Danielson, both established authors of books on shipping. Anthony Cooke has kindly provided other corrections and information, as have many others during discussions that have taken place over the last few years. The help of DP World, Carnival Corporation and Hebridean Cruises plc is gratefully acknowledged.

Nick Robins
Crowmarsh, Oxfordshire
August 2007

I
CRUISING THROUGH TIME

The concept of cruising from Point A and back to Point A purely for the pleasure of the journey is generally credited to the Shetlander, Arthur Anderson. As a boy, Anderson worked on the beaches at Gremista, near Lerwick, and later at Bressay, carrying fish ashore from the boats, gutting, boning, splitting, washing and salting the fish before laying them out to dry. Crop failures and poor fishing ended the boy's schooling but he was looked after by the fish merchant who also saved him on the beach from being taken away by the Press Gang. Later, in 1808, at the age of sixteen, Anderson volunteered for service and became a midshipman aboard HMS *Ardent*. Leaving the Navy in 1815 Anderson next worked as a clerk in London, until he was introduced to his future wife, Mary Ann Hill, daughter of a Scarborough ship owner. It was she who introduced Anderson to the Lime Street shipbroker Brodie McGhie Wilcox.

Anderson was an energetic visionary, who went on to found the Peninsular Steam Navigation Company jointly with Brodie Wilcox in 1834, a company which thrives to this day as the mighty P&O Group, now part of DP World. Anderson also founded the *Shetland Journal*, and in order to fill empty space in the first edition of his newspaper in 1835, he designed a number of spoof advertisements. One of these advertised a two-week sea trip on a mythical steamship to show tourists the wild west coast of Shetland, the Faeroes and Iceland. It was a vision that Anderson was able put in place only nine years later, when P&O began to offer round trips to the Mediterranean and back on a tourist cruise basis.

The tourist sea cruise offered in 1844 was part of a new Indian service. The 'Peninsular', representing the company's original interests in Spain, was shortly followed by the 'eastern Mediterranean', and the 'Oriental', via an overland connection between Suez and Alexandria, ran the west coast of India. The cruise element involved the first leg of this journey to Suez, and was initially provided by the *Great Liverpool* and the *Oriental*, built originally for the Transatlantic Steamship Company in 1837 and 1840 respectively as the *Liverpool* and *United States*.

P&O, which had been formed by the merger of the Peninsular Steam Navigation Company with the Transatlantic Steamship Company in 1840, gave the task of advertising the magic of their cruises to contemporary novelist William Thackeray, who published under the nom de plume Michael Titmarsh. His free passage around the Mediterranean aboard the *Lady Mary Wood* allowed him to see 'as many men and cities as Ulysses surveyed and noted in ten years'. Thackeray was an

The Royal Mail Line's *Atrato* (1853) provides an image of the rigours of steam navigation in the mid-nineteenth century.

intolerant traveller and in today's terms a racist, and he did little to champion the cruise concept. Indeed, his first experience complains about his suffering *mal de mer* in the Bay of Biscay. With the intervention of the Crimean War in 1854 the service was withdrawn.

Despite Arthur Anderson's vision of 1835, the first recorded seaborne excursion was almost certainly that of the wooden steamer *St Andrew*, which took place eight years earlier in 1827. She offered a one-off excursion from Glasgow with overnight accommodation arranged at Londonderry, Tobermory, Fort William and Campbeltown before returning to Glasgow, taking in the sights on the way. The very first proposal for a sea-going pleasure cruise was probably that for the paddle steamer *Francesco*, which had been built in Scotland, and was advertised to carry out a three-month cruise in the eastern Mediterranean in 1833. This was to be 'a voyage which will afford to the learned all the opportunities for the gratification of their laudable curiosity'. The cruise was scheduled to start and end at Naples 'if the number of passengers is sufficient to defray the expenses'. However, no evidence can be found to indicate that the cruise actually took place.

Yet travel by sea was still regarded more as a trial than a pleasure. The Irish author Joseph O'Connor's great novel *Star of the Sea* was first published in the UK in 2002, and describes the awful voyage of Irish immigrants in transit to New York at the height of the Irish Famine in 1847. The story tells of the trials of both tenant farmers and their former landlord crossing from Liverpool to New York. The vision of the stinking, rat-infested steam sailing ship *Star of the Sea*, with her diseased human cargo, more than explains why cruising was not a common pastime at that stage of Queen Victoria's reign.

Pleasure cruising did eventually take off, and once again it was the Scottish coast that was the attraction. Coastal cruises from Liverpool and Ardrossan to the Western Isles were introduced by M. Langlands & Sons in 1870, using the screw cargo and passenger steamer *Princess Royal* which

The *Dunara Castle* (1875) served the Glasgow to Western Isles service for seventy-three years, carrying cruise passengers as far afield as St Kilda in the summer months. (A pen and ink drawing by Donald Meek)

had been built in 1863 for the Liverpool and Western Isles service as part of a through-route to East Coast ports. In 1894, the 1,108-ton gross steamer *Princess Victoria* was built by W. Thompson at Dundee. She was designed specifically for seasonal West Highland cruises and was a finely-appointed ship. The 'tween decks cargo spaces were fitted with temporary cabin accommodation to convert the ships for seasonal 'yachting' duties. Captain McNeill of the *Princess Victoria* reported to Mr Langlands after his first yachting season that, 'the profit on the bar more than covered the expense of the ship and still showed a good round sum on the right side'. He once clipped a rock in the Narrows in the Kyles of Bute, when he found the main channel blocked by a yacht and was forced to take the winding Southern Channel; none of his passengers were aware of the incident!

Because of its proximity to Oban and Mull, Staffa, with its basalt, cathedral-like columns adorning tuneful Fingal's Cave, was already patronised (from the late 1820s) by tourists in steamships, following the example of the artist J.M.W. Turner, the composer Felix Mendelssohn, the poet William Wordsworth and even Queen Victoria. Summer cruises from Glasgow to the Western Isles were offered by Orme Brothers & Company using the newly completed *Dunara Castle* from 1875 onwards, and by John McCallum and Company with the *Hebridean* from 1881 and the *Hebrides* from 1898. The trips were occasionally extended to St Kilda and to Lewis. The *Dunara Castle* plied the route for a remarkable total of seventy-three years, although passenger carrying was discontinued in 1939. There were, however, few other cruise enterprises available during the 1870s and little was heard of deep-sea cruising for a while.

Until the mid-1870s it was customary for passenger shipping companies to include all onboard provisions as part of the fare. Unlimited access to alcohol encouraged passengers to start drinking early in the day, with perhaps a claret at breakfast leading on to spirits later in the day. Holidays and days in port could also allow free champagne, and many passengers were undoubtedly well-oiled for much of the voyage. Once the practice of free booze for all ceased, the passengers had to be given other forms of entertainment. This included concerts (perhaps the steward's band), deck games such as quoits, bull, potato race, tug-of-war, skipping or thread needle races, and games such as chess, whist, euchre and cribbage, as well as a variety of competitions, dances and fancy-dress balls.

Given this ship-board change in attitude, the revival of cruising was brought about by an article published in the *British Medical Journal* in 1880. This recommended sea voyages for their curative powers. The 450-page Pocket Book published by P&O in 1888 (complete with red morocco binding and gilt-embossed covers) for the benefit of would-be passengers, included a long extract from the *BMJ* extolling the newly discovered tonic effect of a voyage to the East. An example is given of a patient who had been 'worn and exhausted by chronic inflammation of the mucous membrane of the lower bowel', the legacy of an attack of dysentery, who recovered the day he left port. But the chief advantage of a P&O cruise was emphatically described as the liberality of the table. And, of course, there was always the tired businessman, congratulated upon eluding, at least for a period, the Post Office and the telegraph wire.

The first dedicated cruise ship was created in 1881 in response to the medics' recommendations. This was the *Ceylon*, of just 2,021 tons gross and built at London in 1858 as one of P&O's pioneer iron-hulled ships, then sold by P&O to John Clark to be adapted for use as a cruising yacht. Two years later, in 1883, she was sold again, this time to the Ocean Steam Yachting Company of Limerick, and marketed under the banner Oceanic Yachting Company. Her routes included round-the-world voyages, but she was mainly used for Baltic and Norwegian destinations. From 1896 she was chartered to the Polytechnic Touring Association. Her ownership changed every few years, and after 1903 the *Ceylon* ended up registered under the ownership of J. Studd of London. Despite this variety, the *Ceylon* remained popular in the cheap cruising yacht role adopted for her by the Polytechnic Touring Association. She was sold for demolition in 1907.

In 1886 the North of Scotland, Orkney and Shetland Company started offering cruises on a more local scale to the Norwegian fjords aboard the *St Rognvald* at £10 per head. Arthur Anderson's vision of cruising to the wild west coast of Shetland, to the Faeroes and Iceland, had indeed become reality. The three-year-old *St Rognvald* normally served the Orkney and Shetland ferry service. The cruises were so well patronised that the North Company built the world's first dedicated cruise ship, the 'steam yacht' *St Sunniva*, in 1887 – she was also the company's first vessel to be equipped with the newly introduced triple expansion steam engine. Rather than displace the *St Rognvald*, the new ship extended the cruising season in subsequent years from May to September, and by 1889 had included Baltic and Mediterranean destinations, the latter on a charter basis.

The success of the Norwegian cruises did not go unnoticed by other companies. The Wilson Line provided similar 'yachting' cruises from Hull to the North Cape and the Norwegian Fjords in the summer months, and to the Mediterranean in the winter months. The Norwegian cruises were operated by the iron-hulled steamship *Domino*, and the Mediterranean services by the *Angelo* and the brand new *Eldorado*. Facilities on the new ship included electricity (the *Domino* and *Angelo* had no such luxury). Berths for seventy-two first-class passengers were located on the Lower Deck, but the seven toilets and two baths were one deck up and shared with thirty-four second-class cruise passengers. The *Eldorado* nevertheless boasted a piano in a small music saloon, a tiny smoking bar and a traditional dining room. Until 1894 any tours ashore had to be organized

The *Garrone* (1873) inaugurated the Orient Line cruise programme in 1889. (National Maritime Museum)

by the individual, but from 1895 onwards shore excursion packages were offered inclusive of hotels and 'victualling'. By 1907, sixteen different tours were available, lasting between nine and twenty-one days.

In 1887 the Edinburgh-based company Salvesen provided direct competition to the North Company out of Leith, with cruises advertised to Norway and the Baltic. That same year the liner companies joined in when both Currie's Castle Line and the Union Steamship Company (later to amalgamate as Union-Castle Line in 1899) each provided a trial Norwegian cruise. Next, in 1889, the Orient Line began offering cruises in both the Norwegian area and to the Mediterranean using the *Garonne*, and from 1891 also the *Chimborazo*, both ships dating from 1871, and both of which had pioneered the company's Australian service. Company advertisements in *The Times* stated that: 'The accommodation for passengers is unsurpassed and their appointments throughout are of the completest character.' The modern era of voyages dedicated solely to the cruise tourist had begun. The *Garonne* was displaced from the service in 1897 by the *Lusitania*, although she was sold two years later after sustaining damage on impact with a jetty at Copenhagen. In July 1899 the *Ophir*, completed only in 1891, took up cruising during her off-season. This first cruise was to Norway and Iceland and the ship was an instant success. So she should have been, as she was luxuriously appointed with a domed three-deck dining room. Her success was short-lived however, as she was chartered out to become the Royal Yacht in 1901 and spent subsequent off-seasons laid up.

In 1893 the beginnings of the Co-operative Cruising Company purchased the nineteen-year-old German liner *General Werder* and renamed her *Midnight Sun*. Under the management of

The *Midnight Sun* (1893) was the first ship operated for the Co-operative Cruising Company. (National Maritime Museum)

Armstrong, Mitchell & Company this vessel provided summer cruises to the Norwegian fjords at budget prices. She could accommodate up to 700 passengers per trip and operated mainly from Newcastle, although the ship was used for trooping during the Boer War from 1899 to 1901.

In 1894 the philanthropist Quintin Hogg founded The Polytechnic Touring Association, with the aim of providing affordable travel for educational purposes by widening the accessibility of travel to the less well-off. The Polytechnic was the Regent Street Polytechnic which Hogg had founded for the education of the poor in that area of London, and which much later became a part of the University of Westminster. The Polytechnic Touring Association chartered the *Cleopatra* from shipbroker P.J. Pitcher of Liverpool. The *Cleopatra* was none other than the former Orient Line cruise ship *Chimborazo*, and she inaugurated the Polytechnic Touring Association programme of cheap cruises to the Norwegian capital and fjords. In 1895 her ownership was transferred to the Ocean Cruising & Yachting Company of London. Age was against the ship, and in 1896 the Oceanic Yachting Company's *Ceylon* was chartered to the Polytechnic Touring Association as a replacement for the *Cleopatra*.

Cruises were also available from Dublin from 1897 onwards when the British & Irish Steam Navigation Company advertised long weekend cruises to Falmouth and Plymouth aboard the *Lady Roberts* and her four sister ships. These little ships normally operated the Dublin to London liner service, and the main concession for cruise passengers was the temporary installation of a piano in the lounge!

The P&O liner *Rome* (1881) later became the cruise yacht *Vectis*.

The realisation that an ocean voyage was no longer a trial of hardship but a pleasurable and memorable experience was the saviour of many passenger liners and indeed their owners. A number of elderly liners were converted specifically for the cruise market in the early twentieth century. Some of the most famous were the twenty-three-year-old P&O liner *Rome*, which became the cruising yacht *Vectis* in 1904, the Caribbean branch liner *Solent* which the Royal Mail Steam Packet converted solely for cruising in the Caribbean in 1905, and their *Ortona*. In 1912 the latter, originally built for the Pacific Steam Navigation Company, became the first of two luxury cruising ships to be given the name *Arcadian*.

The very first purpose-built, ocean-going cruise ship was the German owned *Prinzessin Victoria Luise*, which was completed in 1901 for HAPAG and had a gross tonnage of 4,409. HAPAG had run their inaugural cruise in 1891 when the *Augusta Victoria* was dispatched from Hamburg to the Mediterranean with the first load of German cruise passengers. Unhappily, the *Prinzessin Victoria Luise* was also the first cruise ship to be wrecked. In 1906 she was returning to New York from Jamaica with seventy-four passengers (including three servants) when she ran aground at Port Royal during the night. Ensuing panic was calmed by the ship's officers and all were landed ashore the next morning. However, Captain H. Brunswig assumed full responsibility for the accident, and then shot himself behind his locked cabin door.

By the 1920s the idea that liner off-seasons, the winter on the North Atlantic, and the summer on the Far East routes, could be better utilised by seasonal cruising became widely accepted. The *Laconia* offered the first round-the-world cruise in 1922 on charter to American Express. Cruising also benefited from Prohibition in the USA; the booze cruises out of New York were developed to perfection by the Furness Bermuda Line. In 1925 the Cunard Line brought out their dual summer season liner and winter cruise ship *Carinthia*. That winter she sailed from New York on the first of her round-the-world cruises, featuring forty ports in 142 days, and in later years these were always referred to as her annual 'Millionaires' Cruise'. The last of the cruise yachts, the famous diesel-driven *Stella Polaris*, was commissioned by the Norwegian Bergen Line in 1927. She had a gross tonnage of 5,208 and carried 165 passengers on a one-to-one ratio with the ship's crew.

The *Wilhelm Gustloff* (1937), one of a pair, the first ever cruise ship designed specifically for the mass market, the German Workers' Front, as part of Hitler's 'Strength through Joy' initiative. She suffered the worst ever loss of life at sea when torpedoed in 1940, with the loss of over 5,000 lives.

The Great Depression required many liner companies to look for supplementary employment for their ships. This allowed access to some of the great liners, such as the *Berengaria* (then popularly known as the 'Bargain Area') and the *Mauretania*, for ordinary people who could enjoy a four-day New York cruise to Halifax or Bermuda for a princely $50. These cruises were slotted into the normal five-day layover between liner voyages. Many other ships were given over to full-time cruising whilst others were laid up with canvas covers over funnel tops.

Given the surplus of passenger shipping in the 1930s it is not surprising that there were few ships built for cruising. Nonetheless, Canadian Pacific brought out the magnificent dual-purpose liner and cruise ship *Empress of Britain* in 1931. She had four screws for liner voyages but two of them were removed for the more economical speeds of cruising. The Orient Line initiated the concept of light and airy interiors aboard their new sisters *Orcades* and *Orion*, which were specifically built with a dual liner and cruising role in mind. The very first cruise ships to be purpose built for the mass market were the German *Wilhelm Gustloff* and *Robert Ley*, built in 1937 and 1938 for the Nazi Kraft Durch Freude organisation, Hitler's 'Strength through Joy' scheme for the German Workers' Front. The former was sunk in 1945 by a Russian submarine with the loss of 5,196 lives – the worst-ever recorded loss of life at sea.

A significant dual liner and cruise ship was the Cunard Line's *Caronia*, which was commissioned in 1948 despite post-war austerity. This magnificent luxury liner was designed specifically as a dollar earner and spent much of her early career stationed at New York. Other post-war builds tended to lack innovation and few were designed with the cruise passenger in mind. The North Atlantic liners of Cunard and Canadian Pacific continued to support a winter cruise season, and

The famous Royal Mail Line cruise ship *Atlantis* (1913).

as liner voyages declined in the face of competition from air travel many liners fell back on an increasing cruise ship role.

UK-based cruising provided a salvation for many liners made redundant by the aeroplane. This occurred first on the transatlantic routes, but soon affected all the longer haul services to Asia and Australia. British cruising boomed as it had done in the 1930s. However, the combined effects of the National Seamen's Union strike in 1966, the lifting of personal currency restrictions in the early 1970s and hiked oil prices following the Yom Kippur War saw nearly all the former liners (now with inefficient steam turbine machinery) withdrawn. UK cruising was at an all-time low.

Recovery of the cruising industry required new purpose-built ships and, in due course, these were provided. It was a slow process and many in the mid-1970s believed that the new *Cunard Conquest* (*Cunard Princess*) and *Cunard Countess* would be the very last British-flagged deep-sea passenger ships to be built. How wrong they were, although the Red Ensign is flown on only a fraction of the world's cruise ships today.

By 1965 the largest purpose-built cruise ship was the new Home Lines *Oceanic* under the Panamanian flag, which at 34,000 tons gross featured the first sliding glass roof over the lido area. However, in 1984 innovation returned to Britain when Princess Cruises' *Royal Princess* was launched by Princess Diana. This was the first large cruise ship to offer two decks of cabins, each with their own private verandas. Subsequent economies of scale in the cruise ship industry saw the first of the mega-ships in 1988, when Royal Caribbean commissioned the *Sovereign of the Seas* (73,192 tons gross) at the time the largest passenger ship in the world.

Consolidation of the many independent cruise companies has reduced the number of operators and created fewer, but more powerful, groups. At the dawn of the twenty-first century the Carnival Corporation, based in Miami, controlled the British-flagged and part-British-flagged brands P&O-Princess Cruises, Cunard, Ocean Village and German-targeted Seetours, as well as the foreign-flagged Holland America, Windstar, Costa and Seabourn brands.

Deck cricket on the poop – from the P&O Pocket Book dated 1888.

Cruising has become a major international industry and the ever-expanding modern cruise industry continues its programme of new building to keep pace with demand. Just as the original Suez and Calcutta services of P&O were founded on reliability and the comfort of the passengers, so cruise passengers have become dependent on these same factors. The modern cruise package is sold on the basis that it offers a service scarcely equalled by any land-based hotel, and provides a different shore venue from day-to-day for passengers to enjoy. The contrast with the cruises to St Kilda and Lewis that were enjoyed in the 1870s could not be greater.

SHIPPING COMPANY OFFICIAL GUIDES

From time to time in the late Victorian era, the major passenger shipping lines published official company guides for their prospective passengers. Both P&O and Orient Line guides are typical, while closer to home the ferry and cruise yacht operator David MacBrayne Limited emulated these with its own company guide. Each was produced in hardback with gold tooling, was lavishly illustrated and was available at a modest cost. Today these books are much valued and very collectable.

The third edition of the *Orient Line Guide* was published in 1888 'rewritten with maps and plans'. It was edited by W.J. Loftie, and was available for purchase at half a crown per copy. It was aimed at prospective 'travellers by sea and by land'. The Orient Line was then operating eleven steamers: *Austral*

(5,588 tons gross), *Chimborazo* (3,847 tons gross), *Cuzco* (3,918 tons gross), *Garonne* (3,876 tons gross), *Iberia* (4,702 tons gross), *Liguria* (4,688 tons gross), *Lusitania* (3,825 tons gross), *Orient* (5,386 tons gross), *Ormuz* (6,116 tons gross), *Orizaba* (6,184 tons gross) and *Oroya* (6,184 tons gross). Of these, the *Chimborazo* and the *Garonne* were destined to make a name for themselves as cruise ships (see Chapter 2).

The service was jointly operated with the Pacific Steam Navigation Company, as the guide explains:

> … when in the beginning of 1880, the fortnightly service was determined upon, the Company were fortunate in obtaining the co-operation of the Pacific Steam Navigation Company, whose fine fleet of steamers was in full working order and admirably adapted for the Australian voyage. Troubles at that time breaking out in South America, left the Pacific Company at liberty to devote to the Orient Line the services of a portion of their fleet…

The guide has 360 pages and its contents include engravings of ships and their interiors plus cabin plans of most of the fleet. There are also illustrations of the main ports of call, including some of the monuments and important buildings that can be seen en route to Australia. The book also contains numerous charts and many pages of maps. The text begins with a survey of the medical aspects of the voyage followed by an article on the 'Mother Country'. This is followed by chapters on various segments of the journey.

In comparison to the present-day company promotional video or colourful brochure, the Victorian guides were, if anything, superior. Not just trying to entice you on board for a two-week cruise, they were aimed at selling you the voyage to Australia by the Orient Line or by the P&O Line. As such the old guides provided you with every last detail that you should know before boarding ship. They also left you in no doubt as to whose steamers were the best appointed and the fastest.

TABLE 1: THE KEY PURPOSE-BUILT AND SPECIALLY CONVERTED BRITISH CRUISE SHIPS UP UNTIL THE SECOND WORLD WAR (EXCLUDES VESSELS DEDICATED TO CRUISING IN 1930S BUT WITHOUT IRREVERSIBLE CONVERSION).

Ship	Company	Built	Gross Tons	Comments
Ceylon	J. Clark and other owners	1858	2,021	Sold by P&O in 1881; chartered to Polytechnic Touring Association in 1896
Cleopatra	P.J. Pitcher for Polytechnic Touring Association	1891	3,847	Formerly the Orient Line's *Chimborazo* and used for cruising along with the *Garonne* from 1889 onwards
St Sunniva	North of Scotland, Orkney & Shetland	1887	960	World's first purpose-built dedicated cruise ship
Vectis	P&O	1881	5,548	Built as *Rome*; converted to cruise ship and renamed in 1904
Solent	Royal Mail Steam Packet	1878	1,908	Converted to cruise ship in 1905
The Viking	Polytechnic Touring Association	1881	4,644	Ex-Union Line *Moor* 1901, ex-*La Plata* Royal Mail Steam Packet and converted to cruise ship in 1908

(CONTINUED)

Ship	Company	Built	Gross Tons	Comments
Balantia	Royal Mail Steam Packet	1909	2,380	Built for Caribbean feeder/cruise service
Berbice	Royal Mail Steam Packet	1909	2,380	Built for Caribbean feeder/cruise service
Franconia	Cunard Line	1911	18,150	Built for summer liner duties and winter cruising
Laconia	Cunard Line	1912	18,099	Built for summer liner duties and winter cruising
Arcadian	Royal Mail Steam Packet	1899	8,939	Built as *Ortona*; converted to cruise ship and renamed in 1912
The Viking	Polytechnic Touring Association	1889	5,361	Built as *Atrato* for Royal Mail Steam Packet, sold and converted for cruising in 1912
Fort Hamilton	Furness Bermuda Line	1904	5,530	Ex-*Bermudian*, Quebec Steamship Company 1919
Fort Victoria	Furness Bermuda Line	1912	7,784	Ex-Adelaide Steamship Company 1920
Fort St George	Furness Bermuda Line	1912	7,785	Ex-Adelaide Steamship Company 1920
Arcadian	Royal Mail Steam Packet	1907	12,002	Built as *Asturias*, converted to cruise ship and renamed 1923
Franconia	Cunard Line	1923	20,341	Built for summer liner duties and winter cruising
Araguaya	Royal Mail Steam Packet	1906	11,537	Converted to cruise ship in 1924
Carinthia	Cunard Line	1925	20,270	Built for summer liner duties and winter cruising
Bermuda	Furness Bermuda Line	1927	19,086	Purpose-built
Atlantis	Royal Mail Steam Packet	1913	15,135	Built as *Andes* for Pacific Steam, commissioned by Royal Mail, converted to cruise ship and renamed in 1929
Arandora Star	Blue Star Line	1929	15,178	Built as *Arandora*, converted to cruise ship and renamed in 1929
Empress of Britain	Canadian Pacific	1931	42,348	Built for summer liner duties and winter cruising
Monarch of Bermuda	Furness Bermuda Line	1931	22,424	Purpose-built
Voltaire	Lamport & Holt	1923	13,248	Converted to cruise ship in 1932
Vandyck	Lamport & Holt	1922	13,233	Converted to cruise ship in 1933
Queen of Bermuda	Furness Bermuda Line	1933	22,552	Purpose-built
Orion	Orient Line	1935	23,696	Built for liner duties and cruising
Orcades	Orient Line	1937	23,456	Built for liner duties and cruising

2

EDWARDIAN GRANDEUR

Quoits give a good deal of fun, as the rolling of the vessel, and sometimes the wind, have to be allowed for, and the best player ashore is not always the best afloat. Shovel-board, or shuffle board, is generally popular and can best be described as a halfway game between shove halfpenny and curling. Those who like something more boisterous can indulge in the events of the gymkhana, which usually provoke screams of laughter from start to finish.

From *The Wonder Book of Ships* (Ward, Lock & Co. Ltd), undated.

The constraints and inhibitions of the Victorians were finally replaced with the aspirational grandeur of the Edwardians. Big was definitely beautiful. The big and grand scenery of the fjords overtook the more gentle coastlines that Scotland could offer. The country house style of yachting cruise also overtook the converted make-do ferry, and even Cunard's grand *Lusitania* and *Mauretania* were overtaken by the White Star Line's great and 'unsinkable' Olympic-class liners. The aspirational grandeur of the Edwardians believed that the 'practically unsinkable' *Titanic* protected them in a sublime offshore world, little understanding that their engineers had first to protect the *Titanic*. The Edwardian era was a 'we have come of age' world.

Only months before the coronation of King Edward VII (1901–1910), the North Company's *St Rognvald*, that had given pleasure to so many cruise passengers, was wrecked in fog on passage between Lerwick and Kirkwall. This steam ferry had inaugurated the Norwegian cruises from Scotland, although these had become so popular by 1900 that they were serviced by a number of ferry and liner companies. Thereafter the company's purpose-built cruise ship *St Sunniva* continued to offer cruises to Norway, plus end-of-season round Britain cruises, until she was retrenched to ferry duties in 1908 in the face of intense competition from the other cruise providers.

It had become clear from the Scottish company's advertising literature that it was very conscious of the competition. The 1898 brochure advertised ten-day Norwegian fjord trips at £15 for a single cabin and £8 10s sharing in a four-berth cabin, and continued with the text:

The vessels of this company were the first to begin cruises between Scotland and Norway, and are a convenient size to safely navigate the coast and fjords. The saloons, which are light and airy, are lighted

The *St Sunniva* (1887) was the world's first purpose-built cruise ship. (Aberdeen Maritime Museum)

by electricity. Hot and cold baths are provided. A full staff of stewards and stewardesses are carried, and the cuisine is equal to that of a first-class hotel. A Superintendent accompanies each vessel and arranges for the shore excursions, so as to relieve passengers of personal troubles.

The 'passage money' included all meals and:

Liqueurs may be had from the Steward as per list between 8 a.m. and 11 p.m., when all lights are extinguished, and the pantry closed.

From 1900 onwards the longer Baltic and Northern Cape cruises were dropped in favour of shorter fjord cruises. These were largely operated from Leith, although one ran from Tilbury in 1902. The *St Sunniva*, meanwhile, was equipped with a steam launch to land and collect passengers, and passengers were given the option of longer holidays incorporating a stopover until the ship returned two weeks later. The end-of-season around Britain cruise remained popular to the last, usually sailing from Gravesend to Leith via a variety of ports, including Torquay, Plymouth, the Isle of Man and Dublin.

On the West Coast the success of the pioneer cruise service offered by M. Langlands & Sons, from Liverpool and Ardrossan to the Western Isles of Scotland during the late Victorian era, was demonstrated by the arrival of the 140-passenger *Princess Maud* in 1901, the quasi-sister *Princess Alberta* in 1905 and the 200-passenger *Princess Royal* in 1912. They all had electric lighting throughout and possessed ornately-panelled saloons, whilst much of the first-class cabin accommodation was removable in winter to provide additional cargo stowage. These ships were lost in war, and cruising from Liverpool to the Scottish Isles did not resume thereafter until

Langland's *Princess Maud* (1901) leaving Oban complete with cruise yacht awning on the Promenade Deck aft.

1922 (see Chapter 6). However, Glasgow-based summer cruises to the Western Isles continued unabated, with the *Hebrides* and *Dunara Castle*, as a bonus to their year-round passenger and cargo service to numerous remote island communities (see Chapter 1), as well as the famous cruise programme sustained by David MacBrayne Limited with the cruise yacht *Chieftain*.

On a more grand scale were the Union Line's yachting cruises to Hamburg, Antwerp and Rotterdam, which started running in 1894 from Southampton and were a huge success. These were continued by the Union-Castle Line, although suspended for the duration of the Boer War at the turn of the century when all spare tonnage was required for troop movements. Business was slack after the war, and in 1902 fifteen ships were laid up at Netley in Southampton Water, whilst only nine ships maintained the weekly mail service. When the new *Kenilworth Castle* was commissioned in 1904, the *Dunvegan Castle* was displaced to undertake a programme of cruises to Norway, the Mediterranean and around Britain, before joining the others at Netley before the year was out.

It is from this time onwards that a keen interest was developed in cruising to the sun. Cruises so far had been aimed at admiring the scenery and studying the local people, starting with St Kilda and progressing on to Norway. Next came interest in the sun-filled cruise with Africa and the Caribbean becoming popular destinations, although still very much based on sight-seeing. The *Dunottar Castle*, built in 1890, illustrates this trend, having operated a number of cruises to Norway and the Mediterranean in 1909 under charter to the Sir Henry Lunn Travel Organisation; she even took a large party to the Delhi Durbar in 1911. However, in 1913 she forsook the lilac grey hull of the Union-Castle Line to become the black-hulled and later all white-hulled cruise ship *Caribbean*, based at Barbados for the Royal Mail Steam Packet Company as an extension to the liner service from London. She was later lost in the First World War when she foundered in poor weather conditions off Cape Wrath.

For many years the little excursion ship *Princess Louise* (1898) capitalised on the Western Isles cruise dream by offering day excursions from Oban.

The Union-Castle Line's *Dunottar Castle* (1890) was a dedicated cruise ship from 1909, and in 1913 became the Royal Mail Steam Packet's cruise ship *Caribbean*.

Other pioneers in the new and sunny cruise market were the Orient Line, which had been developing the cruise since the 1890s, and P&O. Both companies started with Scandinavian cruises and then looked further afield to provide sunshine cruises to the Mediterranean and the Caribbean. A typical Orient Line cruise itinerary was a two-month voyage from London via Madeira, Tenerife and Bermuda to a selection of Caribbean destinations. Such cruises were aimed at the very rich and illustrate the ample leisure time that was available to such people.

The Orient Line featured the *Cuzco* in full-time cruising from 1902 until her withdrawal in 1905. The *Ophir* stayed in the cruising market until the onset of the First World War in 1914. A two-week cruise to the Norwegian fjords was at that time priced at between £14 and £20.

In 1903 the Bucknall Line made a series of experimental weekly cruises from Cape Town to Saldhana Bay, each lasting a little longer than a weekend. These were the first South African cruises, but were aimed as much at the British sunshine traveller via the liner service as they were at the South African market. They were not a success and were terminated after six months; could the Edwardian cruise passenger have preferred the grandeur of the dedicated cruise ship rather than the real world of the liner voyage plus added cruise?

Even the Elder Dempster Line joined in through their newly acquired North Atlantic subsidiary, the Beaver Line. Finding the former Norddeutscher Lloyd liner *Ems*, now the Beaver Line's *Lake Simcoe*, surplus to requirements by 1903, she was sent cruising to earn her keep. Whilst the assets of the Beaver Line had been bought by the Canadian Pacific Railway, the *Lake Simcoe* was not included in the deal and was left under Elder Dempster management. Built in 1884, she could not be considered old when she made her debut as a cruise yacht. Nevertheless, she was laid up throughout 1904 and sold to the breakers the following year, allegedly suffering serious mechanical problems. She had carried out a single trial cruise before the sale of the Beaver Line, sailing from the Tyne on 26 July 1902 for Odde, Molde and Stavanger, and spent much of 1903 cruising. However, the success or otherwise of her cruise programme is not recorded.

The era of the grand yachting cruise was exemplified by the P&O cruise yacht *Vectis*. Built in 1881 as the liner *Rome*, and equipped to carry 187 first-class and forty-four second-class passengers, she underwent transformation into a cruise yacht in 1904. She was put on a programme of ten cruises in her first year 'carrying passengers round a given route, calling at various ports and bringing them back to their port of embarkation'. Her first cruise was to Bergen and the Far North, the fare being 35 guineas for a four-week trip. Thereafter, the 'cruise yacht' *Vectis* carried up to 160 first-class passengers, largely on trips to the Baltic and Norway, the Holy Land, Constantinople and the Adriatic, the Canaries and Algiers. She also inaugurated the concept of the 'fly-cruise', with an overland connection rather than by air, from Marseilles returning via Genoa, Naples, Sicily, Malta, Algiers, a Spanish or Portuguese port and then home to London. She was always well maintained and was run with naval smartness. So successful was the *Vectis* that supplementary cruises were offered seasonally by larger capacity ships such as the *Caledonia* and *Mantua*, built in 1894 and 1909 respectively, the *Mantua* having been built at a cost of £308,000. The *Vectis* was sold in 1912 for the paltry sum of £12,500 and later scrapped.

In 1905 the Royal Mail Steam Packet Company similarly converted the smaller steamship *Solent* for 'cruise yacht' duties out of Barbados. With the *Eden* and *Esk*, the *Solent* had operated the 'Intercolonial Service' in the Caribbean as a feeder route for the mainline New York and UK liner services. The local service was advertised for round-trip passengers from 1895. A sixty-five-day

The *Orama* (1911) was designed for the Orient Line with off-season cruising in mind, but was lost in the First World War.

Interior of the first-class public lounge.

Interior of the first-class music room.

Interior of the first-class dining saloon.

The *Solent* (1878) varied her route at the discretion of the passengers when she became a dedicated cruise yacht in 1905.

tour from Southampton, including the Intercolonial Service, cost just £65. The *Solent* was a handsome clipper-bowed steamer built in 1878 and of a modest 1,908 tons gross. She was based at Barbados, and her captain had the discretion to vary his route according to the desires of his passengers on a select-your-own-itinerary basis. With accommodation for 150 first-class passengers, the dedicated 'cruise yacht' was given both a white hull, instead of workaday black, and a ship's orchestra. She was still based at Barbados, and for the next four years operated as the very first Caribbean cruise liner before she was sold for demolition. Connections were available to New York and Europe at the start and end of each cruise via the liner service.

The *Solent* was replaced in 1909 by the white-hulled sisters *Berbice* and *Balantia*. These were larger ships with a gross tonnage of 2,380, and could accommodate 100 first- and fifty second-class passengers. These ships featured electric fans in all the cabins and all the portholes had special shutters to screen the sunlight. The dining saloon was on the main deck and occupied the full width of each ship. In due course they both received mainmasts and black hulls in recognition of their increasing use on liner runs between Kingston and New York after the big cruise ship *Caribbean* had arrived on duty in 1913. At the onset of the First World War the *Berbice* and *Balantia* became hospital ships. The feeder/cruise service was not resumed after the war and the pair were sold in 1922.

Nearer to home, the concept of luxury in the country house style was promoted in 1908 and 1909 when the newly completed liner *Amazon* undertook a series of eleven- to seventeen-day cruises to the Norwegian fjords. Much use was made during these voyages of the ship's boats, which provided excursions to local places of interest. The *Amazon* was succeeded in 1910 by the *Avon* with a New York season of Caribbean cruises in the late winter season and a summer season of Norwegian cruises out of Grimsby. The choice of the latter port was based on the premise

The *Berbice* (1909) was one of a pair of dedicated Caribbean cruise ships which replaced the *Solent* in 1909.

that the shorter North Sea crossing minimised the risk of encountering rough seas even during the summer months.

Demand for luxury cruising was unabated. In 1912 the Royal Mail Steam Packet's liner *Ortona* was transformed into the luxury cruise ship *Arcadian*. Captain J.H. Isherwood described the conversion in an article which first appeared in *Sea Breezes* in August 1953:

> The conversion job took over a year and it was not until the beginning of 1912 that she appeared again in her new role, the largest and most sumptuous vessel in the world solely employed on cruising. She now carried one class of passenger only, 320 of them, and as they had the use of all the spaces previously accommodating 592 people, it can be seen that she was certainly spacious. All the cabins had bedsteads instead of bunks, there was a gymnasium, an electric laundry, an 11m long tiled swimming pool on the Orlop Deck – it was then the largest afloat – a social hall, a reading room, while the great dining room which extended up through three decks to its dome, was newly decorated and provided with an extensive new lighting system.
>
> Outwardly the ship was extensively altered. Most of her cargo gear was removed and the deck sides below the Promenade Deck were plated in. The short gaffs on her masts were removed and an extra boat was carried each side abreast the bridge.

The inaugural cruise of the *Arcadian* started from Southampton in January 1912, travelled via the Caribbean and ended at New York. Although she had grounded at Cartagena, she was towed off unharmed after two failed attempts, one of which left an American freighter with the tow rope fouling her propeller and beached alongside the cruise ship. The Norwegian cruise seasons were then based at Leith and Grimsby while late summer Mediterranean cruises started from Southampton. The *Arcadian* also served the prestigious New York to Bermuda run during the 1913 and 1914 seasons.

The *Avon* (1907) was used for a number of Edwardian cruises.

Royal Mail's luxury cruise ship *Arcadian* (1899) started life as the Pacific Steam Navigation Company's *Ortona*.

One of the more bizarre cruises for the company was a charter in 1912 of their impressive A-class steamer *Araguaya*, on the River Plate service, by the Thames Yacht Club for a special regatta at Kiel which was also attended by the Kaiser. This was very much a foretaste of cruising as the liner was to become a dedicated cruise ship later in life (see Chapter 4).

The *Baltic* (1904) seen in post-*Titanic* guise with additional lifeboats – the *Baltic* originally only had seven each side.

Cunard chartered out their brand new liner *Caronia* in 1906 for a cruise to the Mediterranean. Interest in cruising having been aroused, the *Franconia*, which was commissioned in 1911, and the *Laconia* in 1912, were both built for the Liverpool to Boston service and for luxury winter cruising to the Mediterranean. They were the first British vessels to be fitted with Frahm anti-rolling tanks. Notwithstanding this luxury, they enjoyed only two full cruising seasons before war broke out. Oddly, the huge White Star Line vessel *Baltic* had been employed on cruising shortly after she was commissioned in 1904. With nearly 900 first- and second-class berths to sell, she was clearly too large for the trade on offer and soon reverted to liner duties. The precedent was that her older sister, the *Celtic*, had previously undertaken a successful five-week cruise from New York to the Mediterranean in 1902. Much later, in 1913, the *Laurentic* and *Megantic* were marketed by the Hotel Belmont Steamship and Travel Bureau in New York for winter cruises to the Caribbean and the Panama Canal.

At the cheaper end of the market, the Co-operative Cruising Company operated the *Argonaut* on cruises to the Norwegian fjords until she was sunk in a collision in 1908. There was no loss of life. She had been built in 1879 and was acquired by the Royal Mail Steam Packet Company as *La Plata* in 1893. The *Midnight Sun* resumed seasonal Norwegian cruises in 1901 (see Chapter 1) following two years in service as the troopship *Princess of Wales* in support of the Boer War. Under the ownership of Armstrong Mitchell & Company she was sold for scrap in 1912 at the age of thirty-eight years, having served as a cruise ship for seventeen of them.

Other Royal Mail Steam Packet liners also became cruise ships. Another, *La Plata*, an elderly and outclassed unit which had been built as the *Moor* for the Union Line in 1881, undertook seven years' service with the Royal Mail Steam Packet Company, mainly as a cruise ship, before being resold to the Polytechnic Touring Association in January 1908. Under their ownership she

The Co-operative Cruising Company's *Argonaut* (1879) was a popular cruise ship until she sank in 1908. (National Maritime Museum)

was renamed *The Viking* and placed under the management of associated company, the Viking Cruising Company of Newcastle-upon-Tyne. The livery was a black hull with a white riband, white upperworks and pale buff funnels. *The Viking* provided accommodation for 364 passengers in one class, with large sections of the 'tween decks converted into cabins. Described as being of second-class standard but at economic prices in order to make travel more widely accessible, she proved a big success with a seasonal programme of cruises to the Norwegian fjords, the North Cape and the Baltic and Scandinavian capitals. Miss V.A. Marshall recalled a 1912 Norwegian cruise aboard *The Viking* in a letter to the editor of *Sea Breezes*, dated February 1963:

> The happy friendly atmosphere on board was something to be remembered. The ship's concerts were most memorable, notably the songs My Dreams and Two Eyes of Grey sung by the chief engineer, Mr Waring. The chief officer, second officer and all the engineers contributed wonderfully to the pleasure of the many passengers from London, the Midlands and the North.

In June 1910 the engine telegraph failed while attempting to anchor in Geiranger Fjord and *The Viking* ploughed on to a gently shelving shingle beach. A hapless selection of the only beach along the whole cliff-lined coast was rewarded by the ship being re-floated three days later without sustaining any serious damage. Nevertheless she survived only two more years in service before she was sold for demolition in 1913.

In 1912 the company bought the *Atrato* from Royal Mail as a replacement for *The Viking*. The *Atrato* was a beautiful vessel of 5,361 tons gross which sported a clipper bow and counter stern, two well-raked funnels and three masts – without yards. She was equipped with electric lighting

The Royal Mail Steam Packet Company's cruise ship *La Plata* (1881) later became the first *The Viking* for the Polytechnic Touring Association.

and hydraulic cargo handling cranes. She commenced service in 1889 for the Pacific Steam Navigation Company and, after one trip to South America, took up station on the Caribbean service on which she remained until 1912, even though she had been acquired by the Royal Mail Steam Packet Company in 1906. The first-class return fare from Southampton to the Caribbean was £25 in 1905. Also given the name *The Viking*, and with only minor alterations to her accommodation of 174 first-, forty-four second- and 320 third-class berths, she emerged from refit at Newcastle as an attractive cruising yacht with affordable accommodation for 280. Again very popular on summer cruises, she was requisitioned at the outbreak of war only to be lost as an armed merchant cruiser in a gale off the west coast of Ireland, presumed to have been mined. So ended the ship management days of the Polytechnic Touring Association. However, the name survives to this day as the 'Poly' in the Lunn Poly Travel organisation.

It was during this period that the Booth Line realised it could attract more revenue by marketing its scheduled service from Liverpool to Brazil 'a thousand miles up the Amazon' to cruise passengers. This was a return to the concept of 'reality cruising' that had first been introduced on the west coast of Scotland by the likes of the *Dunara Castle* and the *Hebrides*, way back in the 1870s, and which allowed cruise passengers to interact with people of particular regions and to observe their customs. The first-class accommodation on the Booth Line ships was highly rated, and the *Anselm* (built in 1905), the *Hilary* (1908) and the *Hildebrand* (commissioned in 1911) all proved very popular on the run. The route was via Oporto, Lisbon, Madeira, Para and then up the Amazon to Manaos. After the First World War the service was carried on alone for some time by the *Hildebrand*, which offered accommodation for 218 first-class and 406 third-class travellers, the latter aimed at Portuguese emigrants to Brazil (see Chapter 3).

The *Atrato* (1889) became the second *The Viking* in 1912.

Another initiative was that by Thomas Cook & Son who organised a four-month-long steamer and train itinerary, which was inaugurated in 1908 with the new liner *Orcoma* in the Pacific Steam Navigation Company fleet. The cost was £300 per head, and the liners did not have to deviate from their normal South America west coast route in any way to accommodate the new service.

Another version of the reality cruise, although this time from the perspective of the ship owner rather than that of the cruise passenger, was the shakedown cruise. This was really a test of a new ship during which the crew discovered how the vessel worked before either she or her crew could be entrusted to join the liner service. Such was the case with the P&O liner *Salsette*, built in 1908 for the Aden to Bombay shuttle service connecting with the Australian service at Aden for the UK. On delivery she was sent to Tilbury where she was open to the public at a shilling a head with the proceeds sent to the Seamen's Hospital. From there she operated two cruises, one lasting two and a half weeks to Amsterdam, Christiana, Copenhagen, Kronstadt, Helsingfors and Kiel. The second lasted four weeks and ended at Marseilles via Gibraltar, Algiers, Corfu, Cattaro, Venice and Sicily. Sadly, at the age of nine, the *Salsette* became the victim of a torpedo attack.

What was life aboard ship like? Awoken by the steward in the morning with a cup of tea and a biscuit, the passenger was allowed time for a stroll around deck before descending to the dining saloon for breakfast. Breakfast was over before 10 a.m., and luncheon was served about 1 p.m. and afternoon tea at 4 p.m., the ship's bugler playing an appropriate fanfare to announce each meal. Dressing for dinner was expected on the yachting cruise, with the ship's orchestra entertaining after dinner and lights out set rigidly for 11 p.m. The deck stewards arranged deck games whilst at sea and there was always the daily gamble on the ship's run. In port a variety of shore trips were arranged, sometimes involving overland travel to the ship's next port. The key to the cruise was its pace, far more leisurely and relaxed than today's passenger could tolerate, let alone expect, with delays to the itinerary commonplace.

The Edwardian period was one of great technical advancement. Whilst the liner companies were striving for greater and greater luxury for their first-class passengers, the engineers were making great strides too. The first steam turbine-driven liners were the *Victorian* and *Virginian*, both Allan Line ships built in 1904. In 1901 the Cunard Line's *Lucania* was their first ship to receive wireless telegraphy equipment, whilst other North Atlantic liners soon followed suit. Eventually the shore station network was extended elsewhere so that P&O and the Royal Mail Steam Packet Company equipped their ships with wireless in 1908 and the Orient Line in 1909. The first ship to be fitted with a prototype direction finder was the *Mauretania* in 1912.

Although sea travel was gradually becoming safer and more comfortable there was still a lot to learn, as the tragic loss of the *Titanic* demonstrated in April 1912. But as the various *Titanic* books and films make clear, life was very pleasant on the first-class decks where passengers could continue to search out the sublime, whereas life in steerage remained austere and basic, and without adequate recourse to life-saving equipment. That being so, the era of luxury travel and deluxe cruises was about to end as the world braced itself for war and the loss and suffering which would inevitably ensue. Britain declared war on Germany in August 1914. This was the war in which the submarine and the mine were deployed in earnest; this was the war in which Britain lost over 9 million tons of shipping.

THE ROYAL MAIL LINE'S *AVON* OF 1907

The fourth of the six Edwardian A-class liners of the Royal Mail Line fleet was the *Avon*. She commenced her maiden voyage from Southampton on 28 June 1907 when she set new standards of luxury on the South American run. She joined the *Amazon*, *Aragon* and *Araguaya*, the first three of the class, and was followed by the *Asturias* and the final ship of the class, the *Almanzora*. Such was the programme of building that by 1910 the *Avon* was seasonally displaced from the liner service to run Caribbean cruises from New York and the UK, whilst Norwegian cruises also featured in her UK cruise programme.

As each ship of the class was delivered, she was hailed as the most luxuriously appointed yet, and the *Avon* was no exception. She offered numerous single berth cabins, several deluxe suites and the public rooms were decorated in a distinctive but exotic style favoured by the Latin meat barons. Balconies, domes, smoke room and grand saloons, as well as a gymnasium, were all highlighted in the company literature as selling points of the ship. However, the luxury of the 'elevator' was still to come and the millionaire passengers still had to take the stairs.

An attractive looking ship, she could accommodate 300 first-class and 130 second-class passengers in varying degrees of luxury. There were also berths for 1,000 steerage-class passengers as calls en route in Spain tapped the two-way flow of migrant workers and the one-way flow of Spanish emigrants bound for the River Plate ports.

At the start of the First World War the *Avon* was occupied with troop movements in the English Channel before being converted to the Armed Merchant Cruiser HMS *Avoca*. Armed with eight 6in guns and two anti-aircraft guns she joined the 15th Cruiser Squadron in the Pacific. Her patrol zone ran all the way from Vancouver down to the Horn. Long and dull it may have been, but it was necessary given the risk of German merchant shipping being converted to raiders in South

American ports. One note of excitement occurred when she was dispatched to Santa Cruz, where the Mexican Governor had decided to seize all British property under cover of war. HMS *Avoca* landed an armed party and in response to an ultimatum regained the assets from the miscreant Governor. The remainder of her war was spent on North Atlantic escort duties and the ship was duly returned to her owners early in 1919, largely none the worse for her wartime adventures.

The *Avon* resumed service to the River Plate later in 1919. However, increasingly subservient to newer tonnage, the *Avon* took on a seasonal cruising role throughout the 1920s, becoming a dedicated cruise ship complete with white hull in 1927 (see Chapter 3). Joined by the *Asturias* (then renamed as the cruise ship *Arcadian*) and the *Araguya*, the three cruise ships carved a niche in the cruising industry during the late 1920s. But, in response to the world slump, the *Avon* was first to be withdrawn and was laid up in Southampton in September 1929, releasing a mere £31,000 on sale to ship breakers the following year. Like her sisters, she is remembered as a comfortable and luxurious Edwardian liner that served her owners equally well as a dedicated luxury cruise ship.

3

OFF-SEASON LINERS AND FULL-TIME CRUISE SHIPS

The 1920s was the period in which the off-season liner was put to luxury cruising, with some notable new builds designed specifically with seasonal cruising in mind. Demand for sunshine cruises was such that a number of liners were also taken out of service and converted for full-time, high-class cruising. However, the cheap mass market cruise was yet to be developed (see Chapter 5).

Many liner trades had a down season – the winter months on the North Atlantic and the summer months on the Australian run. Both Cunard and Canadian Pacific were quick to develop winter cruises to the Mediterranean and the Atlantic Isles, even though there was a shortage of tonnage on the liner routes after the First World War. Cunard took the decision to build two ships, the *Franconia* and *Carinthia*, with dual roles of transatlantic liner and cruise ship, the latter specifically to satisfy the luxury cruise market that was burgeoning in the United States. In addition, the US Government Immigration Restriction Act of 1922 had reduced the emphasis on full-time liner traffic. The two new cruise liners were slightly more luxurious than their three sisters, *Scythia*, *Samaria* and *Laconia*. They had a special sports arena on G-deck occupying the full width of each ship, and they offered a large swimming pool, gymnasium and squash courts. There was also an area set aside for deck games on the Promenade Deck. Nevertheless, the *Samaria* undertook world cruises out of New York in 1923 and 1924, on charter to Thomas Cook & Son, for 600 one-class passengers. She also discharged a number of shorter cruises of up to thirty days as well. The *Scythia* carried out at least one cruise from New York to the Mediterranean in 1923, under charter to the Frank Tourist Company.

Launched from Vickers Armstrong at Barrow-in-Furness in February 1925, the new *Carinthia* made her maiden voyage from Liverpool to New York in August that year. During the winter she sailed from New York on the first of her annual round-the-world 'millionaires' cruises', returning to Liverpool in March – in time to resume liner services. This became a standard pattern for the ship, although a number of summer UK-based cruises, principally to Scandinavia, soon became interspersed between liner voyages.

The *Carinthia* was 190m long and had, by today's standards, a narrow beam of only 22m. Her gross tonnage, as built, was 20,270 and her main power units were twin turbine sets which gave her a service speed of 16 knots. Her passenger accommodation was divided between 330 first-, 460 second- and 950 third-class rooms, although as a cruise ship her passenger complement was

The *Franconia* (1923) is seen in her 'cruising white' livery, adopted in the 1930s.

The Royal Mail Steam Packet Company's *Ohio* (1923) provided off-season cruises until 1927, when she was transferred to the White Star Line fleet as the *Albertic* and later scrapped at the age of only eleven, although she was originally laid-down in Germany in 1913.

significantly reduced. The *Franconia* was also regularly deployed on winter cruising, but unlike her sister these were dominantly UK based. The two ships proved enormously popular with the so-called 'American socialite pleasure seekers'. The 1934 world cruise of the *Franconia* was advertised as a 'voyage of discovery' taking in rarely visited ports in the southern hemisphere. The advertising brochure concluded: 'After all it might not be such a bad idea to try to discover how the other half lives.' The ship carried author and historian Hendrik Willem van Loon as official lecturer for the voyage.

During the 1930s the *Carinthia* was almost entirely dedicated to cruising and received a white hull in recognition of this duty, as did the *Franconia*. The final cruise carried out by the *Carinthia* before the Second World War was from New York to Quebec and Newfoundland, having previously completed a series of New York to Bermuda cruises. Requisitioned for war service, the once majestic and luxurious cruise ship turned armed merchant cruiser HMS *Carinthia* was torpedoed and sunk in June 1940 off the west coast of Ireland whilst on the Northern Patrol. The *Franconia* survived the war and was eventually scrapped in 1957.

The *Lancastria* (laid down as the Anchor Line's *Tyrrenhia*) was converted to a two-class ship in 1924 when she was in Cunard ownership. Adorned with two swimming pools on her Promenade Deck, she also began a dual role of liner and cruise ship. She was a major war casualty, sunk at St Nazaire on 17 June 1940 with the loss of at least 3,000 men.

The Canadian Pacific Line used the *Empress of Scotland* extensively for cruising in the 1920s. Built for HAPAG in 1905 as the *Kaiserin Auguste Victoria*, she was bought by Canadian Pacific in 1921. In January 1922 she emerged from refit – with her new name – for a charter cruise in the Mediterranean, and then left for New York to pick up further passengers for another cruise in the Mediterranean. Every winter thereafter she was employed on cruising, including prestigious round-the-world cruises out of New York in 1925 and 1926 which lasted six months apiece. In 1928 she became the world's largest full-time cruising yacht and was then painted white with a blue riband around her white hull. Her enormous success persuaded Canadian Pacific to build a ship specially for cruising between seasonal liner duties. This was the famous *Empress of Britain* which displaced the *Empress of Scotland* from her cruising role after the 1930 season. The cabin-class *Montroyal*, formerly the 1906-built *Empress of Britain*, also cruised extensively from the UK to the Mediterranean and the Caribbean from the 1924 season onwards.

Canadian Pacific's *Empress of Britain* surpassed even the spaciousness and luxury of the *Carinthia*. The *Empress of Britain* was an attempt by Canadian Pacific to woo Mid- and Far-West American transatlantic passengers away from New York to Quebec and Montreal. To do this, it had to offer serious luxury as well as speed, and when she carried out her maiden voyage in May 1931, only the German liners *Bremen* and *Europa* could outpace her. She provided fabulous accommodation for 452 first-class passengers, and could accommodate a further 250 in tourist and 470 in third class. She was also the first liner to boast a full-size tennis court. But that was not all – she was also designed, like the *Carinthia*, as a winter-season cruise ship. Length and draught were limited by the dimensions of the Panama Canal and this made the ship appear very tall. The funnels were massive, both in height and diameter, in order to balance her profile.

Her two outboard propellers were removed at the start of each winter cruise season for slower but more economical speeds. This gave her a cruise speed of 18 knots, as opposed to 25 knots as a transatlantic liner. Each winter included a round-the-world cruise starting and finishing at New York. The first of these commenced on 3 December 1931 and finished eighty-one ports later on 8 April. This pattern of operation continued throughout the 1930s, culminating in bringing

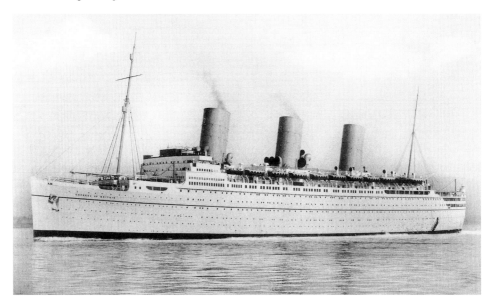

The *Empress of Britain* (1931) in side elevation.

The *Empress of Britain* in the Suez Canal at Ismailia on a cruise.

home King George VI and Queen Elizabeth from their North American tour in 1939. The King reportedly described the ship as, 'the most magnificent ship I have ever seen'. Sadly the majestic liner *Empress of Britain* was lost in 1940 while acting as a troop transport.

There were also some notable conversions to full-time cruise ships. In 1923 the Royal Mail Steam Packet Company's A-class *Asturias* on the River Plate service, which had been built in

Interior of the *Empress of Britain*'s first-class children's playroom.

The *Empress of Britain*'s Mayfair lounge.

1907 and was badly damaged in the First World War, was refitted as the luxury full-time cruise ship *Arcadian*. This was rather a bold move as there was still a shortage of passenger liner tonnage at that time, although the South American trade had become increasingly competitive with both the French and Italians putting more tonnage on the service.

At the end of the war the *Asturias* had been written-off as a constructive total loss and her owners received the insurance payments for her. She was then used as an ammunition hulk for two years at Plymouth. However, the hulk was later bought back by the Royal Mail Steam Packet

The Olympian swimming pool aboard the *Empress of Britain*.

The Cathay Lounge on the *Empress of Britain*.

Company and towed to lay up at Harland & Wolff's yard at Belfast. Eventually, in 1922, as other priorities had been dealt with, the ship was refitted as a two-class luxury cruise ship and converted to burn oil fuel. The gamble was successful and, as the *Arcadian*, she quickly developed a cruise clientele of such size that a second ship was required to satisfy demand.

The second ship was the *Araguaya*, which was converted in 1924 at Harland & Wolff, emerging with accommodation for just 365 first-class cruise passengers. In winter she sailed out of

The Empress Room aboard the *Empress of Britain*.

The *Arcadian* (1907) was operated as a dedicated cruise ship by the Royal Mail Steam Packet between 1923 and 1933, and was formerly the A-class liner *Asturias*.

New York to Cuba, Bermuda or the Caribbean, and in summer she ran UK-based cruises from Tilbury to Norway, and in late summer to the Mediterranean. Less successful than the *Arcadian*, she was sold for further service under the Yugoslavian flag in 1930. In 1929, the *Arcadian* became the first British cruise ship to call at Leningrad, but the old ship was also withdrawn from service the following year and laid up to await sale. The *Avon* was painted white in 1927 when she too adopted the role of the cruise ship, making round-Britain and Norwegian cruises from a variety of UK ports. She was withdrawn and scrapped in 1929.

In early 1926 the elderly *Orca* was chartered to the American Express Company to target the richer British and American market with a long cruise to the Caribbean, the Atlantic Isles and Africa. This was followed in January 1927 when the new motor-driven *Asturias* carried out a 101-day cruise which included extensive overland options. The *Asturias* was typical of the period; the first-class smoke room was decorated in the manner of William and Mary, whilst the dining saloon imitated the style of Christopher Wren.

Another of the pre-war A-class liners, the *Andes*, was converted into a dedicated cruise ship and renamed the *Atlantis* in 1929. The *Andes* had been built for the Pacific Steam Navigation Company but commissioned by the Royal Mail Steam Packet in 1913 along with sisters *Alcantara* and *Almanzora*. The ships had triple screws, with triple expansion engines driving the wing shafts, and exhausting into a low pressure turbine on the central shaft. Their service speed was 17 knots. The first-class passenger accommodation was the finest of the day and, as built, there were ample third-class berths for Portuguese and Spanish emigrants. With collapsible furniture these berths were often converted into hold space for the return journey. Intriguingly the *Andes* was one of the very first liners to be armed in peacetime, with two 4.7-inch guns placed right aft.

The *Andes* served the River Plate route until 1914 when she was requisitioned as an armed merchant cruiser. Her war career included the sinking of the German raider *Greif* in company with the *Alcantara*, a battle which saw the loss of the *Alcantara* as well as the raider.

Peacetime gave the *Andes* another ten years on the River Plate service until the new 22,000-ton motor liners, the new *Asturias* and *Alcantara*, arrived on the scene. Eclipsed by the new ships and with the onset of the Depression, the *Andes* was withdrawn and sent to Gladstone Dock in Liverpool for conversion to a luxury cruise ship. Her accommodation was rebuilt for just 450 passengers, and she was converted from coal to oil burning, emerging with a white hull under the new name *Atlantis*. For the next four years she undertook a variety of luxury cruises to the Baltic, the Norwegian fjords, the Mediterranean and the Caribbean, as well as longer cruises round South America via the Panama Canal and the Magellan Strait, South Africa and Panama to Hawaii and the Pacific Islands.

In 1933 the *Atlantis* was given another extensive refit which enabled her to continue in service until the outbreak of war. She featured seven-day cruises for just 11 guineas, and at the top of the range were twenty-two-day cruises to the Baltic for 300 guineas. In 1936 she offered a fifty-eight-day African cruise at prices starting from 120 guineas. However, the *Arcadian* became too expensive a unit to maintain and was withdrawn and sent to the breakers' yard, having served as a cruise ship for the previous ten years. The *Atlantis* later served as a hospital ship and ended her days as a post-war emigrant ship travelling to Australia and New Zealand, being dispatched to the ship breakers only in 1952 at the grand age of thirty-nine.

Ironically, the new motor ships that had displaced the former *Andes* from the River Plate service had to be re-engined with steam turbine engines to counter poor speed and serious vibration problems. In 1934 the newly re-engined *Asturias* was sent on another extensive cruise from Southampton via the Mediterranean to the Caribbean and to the South Pacific before being re-entrusted with the River Plate liner service.

Perhaps the most celebrated conversion was the Blue Star Line's *Arandora Star*. She was built as one of a class of five refrigerated cargo and passenger liners for the Vestey Brothers' Blue Star Line to inaugurate a new fortnightly service out of London to the River Plate and Vestey's meat

The *Arandora Star* (1927) seen in an early state of modification about 1931.

The *Arandora Star* again in 1935.

interests in Argentina. At 12,850 tons gross these vessels had useful cargo space with three holds fore and three aft of the accommodation, but also provided luxury first-class accommodation for 164 passengers. The boilers were oil-burning but coal could be utilised instead, and the twin turbines drove the ships on an eighteen-day passage via intermediate ports to Buenos Aires (the city's name literally means 'good airs', compared to the tropics to the north). It is interesting to note that the Vesteys put £300,000 into the project from their personal funds to ensure that the

The *Arandora Star* minus mainmast, seen at Tarragona.

The ballroom aboard the *Arandora Star*.

order for building the five passenger ships, plus four more cargo vessels, was placed with UK yards. The total cost of the nine ships was £3.5 million.

The passenger accommodation aboard the five sisters was set on the theme of an eighteenth-century English country house. There were parquet floors, fluted columns, fine carpets and silk furnishings with pastel shades providing a lightness to the public rooms that was before its time. The dining room was forward between numbers 2 and 3 holds on the main deck, and could seat all the passengers at one sitting. The smoke room and veranda café were aft and the lounge forward on the Promenade Deck. The staterooms (there were no cabins) were all outside and offered beds rather than bunks. The new service commenced in February 1927 with the maiden voyage of the *Almeda*, followed by the *Avila*, *Andalucia* and *Avelona*, and by June the last of the quintet, the *Arandora*, had joined the service. They were all given a Star suffix to their names in due course to avoid confusion with the Royal Mail A-class liners.

Within a year of the new service starting, the Blue Star Line was accepted into the South America freight conference, providing the company with outward cargoes but reducing the number of ships required in the composite service that was then created. After only eight round trips the *Arandora* was withdrawn and in January 1929 arrived at Fairfield's Govan yard for conversion, at a cost of £200,000, into a luxury cruise ship with accommodation for 354 passengers.

The five-month-long refit of the *Arandora Star* included lengthening of the superstructure fore and aft with extra cabins on the bridge deck and an extended dining room. The other public rooms were enlarged and a new ballroom incorporated aft of the veranda café. These alterations allowed a small games deck to be installed forward, with a larger games area on the upper Promenade Deck. There was a gymnasium and a passenger lift, and to top this all the steam-driven deck machinery was replaced with electric equipment. This refit was completed on 25 May, and the cruise ship *Arandora Star* was placed under the command of Captain Edgar Moulton.

Her inaugural promotional cruise was a one-day English Channel cruise for a princely 35 shillings per head. This was followed by open days at London, thence to Immingham to commence a series of Norwegian cruises. The Mediterranean season was in spring and autumn and the Caribbean in winter. In the early winter of each year she was taken in hand for refit and modification. In 1931 she received an all white cruising livery and her derrick posts were removed. The following year thirty-nine new cabins were added to the Promenade Deck forward and a new games deck added above, making her look a little top heavy.

In 1934 the *Arandora Star* transferred her Norwegian departures to Tilbury and made her first sortie to the Pacific via the Panama Canal. These cruises, which were repeated in 1936 and 1937, took in Hawaii, Los Angeles and San Francisco. Further conversion included the removal of the mainmast in 1936 to reduce rolling, the construction of a large swimming pool and minor adjustments to create features such as card rooms. In 1935 her hull band, which had been red, was changed to green following the winter refit in January 1935. In these new colours she set sail from Southampton on a three-month winter cruise to South Africa, Java, Malaya, Ceylon (Sri Lanka) and returned via Suez and the Mediterranean. Final alterations took place in 1937 when the Promenade Deck was extended almost to the bow. There were two elegant galleries installed between the smoking room and the lounge and a new cocktail bar replaced the writing room aft. At this time her green hull band became blue. All this additional top hamper required ballasting and her loaded draft had increased from 8.4 metres as built to 8.6 metres by 1939.

On 26 August 1939 the *Arandora Star* arrived back at Southampton at the end of her very last cruise – number 124. She was shortly to sail to the United States with American personnel. The ship was lost in 1940 to a German torpedo. She had been carrying 565 German and 734 Italian internees to Canada – 805 people died in the incident, including Captain Moulton, who had been with the ship since 1929.

The last of the four-masted Bibby Line ships was the *Derbyshire* (1935), offering tourist trips to the Mediterranean and beyond.

The Pacific Steam Navigation Company had not been involved with cruising in the early days. However, a group of its ships were taken into Royal Mail ownership and very quickly the *Orduna* was used to provide a Welsh-speaking cruise in 1922. Used on North American routes, the ships were returned to the Pacific Steam Navigation Company for their South America west coast service in 1927. Between 1923 and 1927, the *Orduna*, along with the *Ohio*, *Orca* and *Orbita*, provided a series of off-season winter cruises as tourist-class ships.

The White Star Line reverted to winter cruising in the 1920s, using ships such as the high-passenger capacity *Adriatic* from 1926 onwards. The White Star Line was bought back into British ownership from the American-owned International Mercantile Marine Company in 1927 by Lord Kylsant's Royal Mail Group. In order to raise the capital Lord Kylsant had a new company incorporated as White Star Line Limited – upsetting the IMM in doing so as they still owned the White Star Line – and issuing two and a half million £1 shares. The issue was grossly oversubscribed and a further issue was made some months later. An additional £4 million in share capital was subscribed by the Royal Mail Steam Packet Company but only at a rate of 2/- for each £1 share. This led to the eventual imprisonment of Kylsant when the under-funding was uncovered in 1931, and the inevitable end of the White Star Line which by 1930 was, for the first time in its history, running at a loss. When the Royal Mail Steam Packet Company finally went bust in 1936 the time was ripe for a merger of the White Star Line with the Cunard Line (see Chapter 5).

The Orient Line continued to offer cruises throughout much of the 1920s. These resumed after the war in 1921 using the war-reparation Norddeutscher Lloyd steamer *Zepperlin*, bought in 1920 by the Orient Line and renamed *Ormuz*. She was seen as stop-gap tonnage and was sold in 1926. The *Ormonde*, *Oronsay*, *Orsova* and *Orama* also regularly made off-season cruises to the Norwegian fjords and the Mediterranean, and in 1928 the *Ormuz* carried the Marine Biological Association

The *Ormonde* (1917) at anchor during a Norwegian cruise.

Orient Lines *Otranto* (1925) inaugurated calls at Majorca to boost passenger numbers during her regular liner voyages.

on a mammoth expedition to the Great Barrier Reef. The new *Otranto* was also extensively engaged in cruising, principally to the fjords, the Western Isles of Scotland, the Mediterranean and occasionally also to the Caribbean. She was severely damaged when she grounded off Greece in 1926 during a 'battlefields of Gallipoli cruise', later returning to the UK under her own

The *City of Paris* (1921) ran popular North Sea cruises in between liner voyages.

steam for repairs. She also suffered a head-on collision with a Japanese freighter having just left Immingham for a Norwegian cruise. The dining saloon was a scene of pandemonium when the Japanese vessel swung after impact and slammed alongside the *Otranto*. Injuries were fortunately slight; the ship was able to return to Immingham and the passengers were sent home in a series of hastily-chartered trains bound for Manchester, London and Glasgow.

The Orient Line also operated New York-based cruises to Norway using the *Osterley*. These took place in 1922 with the ship under charter to an American travel company.

The Ellerman Line introduced the *City of Paris* to their Far Eastern routes in 1921. However, they quickly found better employment for her in the off-season with a series of North Sea cruises using the 255 first-class berths that were available, whilst her older consorts carried on the liner service throughout the year. Described as 'lightly decorated and homely', the *City of Paris* returned to cruising again in the 1930s (see Chapter 5).

Several liner companies actively advertised their regular services as round trip cruises in the 1920s and 1930s. In 1911 the Harrison Line had acquired the Aberdeen Direct Line, managed by John Rennie Son & Company. Of the seven Aberdeen Direct Line ships, two were passenger liners, the *Inanda* and *Intaba*, dating from 1904 and 1910 respectively, engaged in the UK service to Natal, South Africa. They were joined in 1913 by a third passenger liner, the *Ingoma*, but the three ships were switched to more traditional Harrison Line trade between London and the Caribbean after the First World War, when they quickly became very popular with round trippers. A new *Inanda* was commissioned in 1925 with accommodation for ninety-one first-class passengers, and she eventually ran in a two-ship service when the new *Inkosi* was delivered in 1937, offering excellent first-class accommodation for eighty-two passengers. The service was not resumed after the Second World War.

Elders & Fyffes carried passengers on their 'banana boats', running in competition with the Harrison Line, until after the Second World War. In the 1930s it was possible to take the round

The Harrison Line Caribbean service was championed by the *Inanda* (1925) for many years. Raised after a bombing raid in the Second World War she was renamed *Empire Explorer*.

Harrison Line's *Inkosi* (1937) had barely eighteen months on the Caribbean service before the Second World War. Raised after a bombing raid in the war – like her running mate the *Inanda* – she later became the cargo-only *Planter*.

trip with three nights ashore in a good hotel for £45. However, as Rotterdam was the European terminal, UK passengers were uplifted at Dartmouth until a new banana berth was commissioned at Southampton in 1931. Three new ships were delivered for the service in the 1920s: the *Cavina*, *Carare* and *Ariguani*, each with one-class (first-class) accommodation for 100 passengers. These

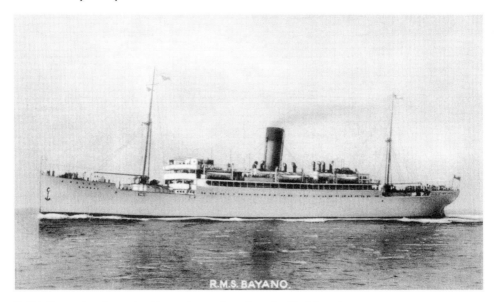

Fyffe's *Bayano* (1915) remained in service until 1956 on the Caribbean banana run.

ships joined the *Bayano*, *Coronado* and *Camito* dating from 1915–17, whilst the *Patuca* was reduced to a spare passenger ship with berth numbers reduced to only fifty. The *Coronado* was sold for demolition in 1935, whilst the other five continued on until 1939. The *Cavina*, *Bayano* and *Ariguani* survived the war and continued in service until the mid-1950s, when they were replaced with new tonnage.

Another service that was popular with the round-trip brigade was the Yeoward Brothers' Liverpool to the Canary Islands service. Yeoward's popularity peaked in the mid-1930s. The route was then maintained by the *Ardeola*, *Aguila*, *Alondra*, *Avoceta* and *Alca*, the latter with accommodation for over 200 passengers. From 1938 onwards the Liverpool to Canary Island service was pooled with MacAndrews & Company and their fleet of modern motor ships with accommodation for just twelve passengers.

The very distinctive three-masted ships of the Yeoward Brothers' fleet were built between 1912 and 1927, and the largest was only 3,700 tons gross. Sailing day was usually Saturday, when the ships moved from their berth at North Coburg Dock to receive passengers either alongside Princes Landing Stage or in mid-river via a tender. The *Avoceta* also ran occasion cruises from the UK to Norway in the late 1930s. The *Alondra* was sold in 1939, and of the others the *Alca* alone survived the war but she was withdrawn in 1954, ending the passenger service.

The round-Africa circle route was reinstated in 1922 by the Union-Castle Line. This service was always very popular with tourist traffic, and continued to be so up until the Second World War.

For its part, the Bibby Line began to advertise tours in the latter half of the 1920s. Their classic four-masted liners ran to Gibraltar, Marseilles, Port Said, Sudan, Ceylon (Sri Lanka) and southern India, the so-called Straits Settlements and Burma. Summer itineraries centred on 'Mediterranean and Continental tours' and used Gibraltar and Marseilles as bases, while winter tours were either centred on Egypt or beyond to Sudan or Ceylon. The Mediterranean cruise passengers helped boost cabin numbers left vacant by long-distance passengers preferring the faster overland option between Marseilles and Britain. These tourist operations helped to provide revenue for the

The flagship of the Yeoward Line was the *Alca* (1927), always popular on the Canary Islands circuit.

company during the hard-pressed years leading through the 1930s and were extremely popular. Although Sri Lanka remains a popular holiday destination to this day, an eight or nine-week sail through the Suez Canal to Colombo and back contrasts with the modern preferred option of a nine-hour flight. It also highlights the leisure time available to what was then described as England's upper-middle classes.

The 'thousand miles up the Amazon' cruises of the Booth Line (see Chapter 2) were continued after the First World War by the *Hilderbrand* throughout the 1920s. Occasional calls were made to Caribbean destinations as further incentive for round-trip passengers from 1925 onwards. The *Hilary* replaced the *Hilderbrand* in 1931. The *Hilary* proved just as popular, with first-class accommodation for eighty, including four deluxe staterooms with private bath and toilet, and there were third-class berths for a further 250. She was joined by a similar ship, the *Anselm*, in 1935. The first-class drawing room and lounge were forward on the Promenade Deck; the smoking room and veranda café were at the after end. The dining saloon could seat ninety-two and was situated on the main deck.

A BUSINESS OF NATIONAL IMPORTANCE

The downfall of Lord Kylsant and his Royal Mail Group of companies, probably the world's largest ship owners at the time, is described in *A Business of National Importance* by Green and Moss. The Royal Mail Group was so important to Britain that when the Bank of England realised there were serious financial problems it stepped in to assist in salvaging what it could. The Royal Mail Group's Harland & Wolff shipyard in Belfast was vital to the newly formed Northern Ireland and the Government could not afford for the yard to be bankrupted and closed. The building of the big motor

---

ships *Asturias* and *Alcantara* for parent Royal Mail Steam Packet Company had cost Harland & Wolff dearly, as full and prompt payment for them was not made.

The prospectus for the building of the *Asturias* and *Alcantara* during the 1920s had alerted the Bank of England to financial malpractice within the Royal Mail Group. New ships for group members were ordered from the company-owned shipyards but there was little money available to pay the bills. When Kylsant undertook to buy the White Star Line back from the American-owned International Mercantile Marine, both he and 'his wonderful web of deceit' were exposed. A leading firm of accountants, Thomson McLintock & Company of Glasgow, was appointed by the Bank of England to unravel the web and put the Royal Mail interests back on the rails.

The Government could not afford the shipping empire to collapse. A key to the reorganisation of the group was the settlement of claims in American courts over the loss of the Royal Mail Group's Lamport & Holt Line's *Vestris* outside New York harbour in November 1928, with the loss of 112 lives. This work was finalised in 1933, but not before the *Voltaire* was able to resume business as a cruise ship following the withdrawal from the prestigious New York route. With this settlement in place, the sale of the various component parts of the Royal Mail Group was possible, leading up to the formation of the Royal Mail Line following the eventual collapse of the Royal Mail Steam Packet Company. There were also a lot of vessels that normal business practice would never have ordered, had the Royal Mail Group not corporate shipyards to support, and many modern ships as well as whole companies were sold to bolster the finances.

Lord Kylsant is always painted as a rogue for allowing his empire to fall into financial ruin. It is more likely that he was a victim of his own business success and the complexity of large groups of companies such as Royal Mail. His problems also reflected the relatively lax financial regulations then in place. Aware of this, the Government ordered a thorough audit of the P&O group of companies in 1932, fearful that Lord Inchcape could be in charge of a similarly under-financed complex of shipping interests. The work was carried out by Deloite, Plender, Griffiths & Company, and although the value of many of the assets was considerably written down, P&O was found to be on a more secure financial foundation.

The survival of both the Royal Mail and P&O groups of shipping companies was vital to the nation in the 1930s. They would soon provide a core transport service to the island nation in the Second World War and were the carrier of much of the trade in the post-war years in the twilight of the Empire. In the meantime, both the Royal Mail Line and the remnants of the Lamport and Holt Line, along with P&O and its associate companies, provided a large part of the UK cruising opportunities in the 1930s and thereafter.

4

PROHIBITION

Popularity [of cruising] was undoubtedly enhanced by Prohibition in the United States. The prospect of cheap booze in a British ship and a spell in a pleasant holiday island with drinks as required was a tremendous inducement to thirsty Americans.

From an article by J.H. Isherwood which first appeared in *Sea Breezes*, April 1973.

Cruising, in this case cruising to and from a holiday destination, was given a considerable boost with the introduction of Prohibition in the United States in 1919. Prohibition was the result of a prolonged campaign by church and women's organisations, temperance societies and the Anti-Saloon League. However, it led to bootlegging which was largely carried out by organised crime syndicates and Prohibition was finally repealed in 1933. For thirteen years the United States was ostensibly dry, and cruises aboard foreign-registered ships to nearby but foreign destinations, such as Bermuda and the Caribbean, became extremely attractive.

Although a number of British liner companies took advantage of the thirsty American market for off-season cruises out of New York, Furness Withy created an entirely new shipping company. This company was wholly dedicated to valuable dollar earning and to the sale of alcohol. Just as the American Matson Line developed cruises to the company-owned Royal Hawaiian Hotel during the 1920s, so Furness Withy developed cruises to company-owned hotels in Bermuda. Furness Withy saw the potential of the route when they bought the Quebec Steamship Company, their interests in the New York to Bermuda trade and their twin-funnelled steamer *Bermudian* in 1919. She had been built in 1904 and was of modest proportions, being some 5,530 tons gross. Furness Withy renamed her *Fort Hamilton*, fitted her out with first-class accommodation and installed several new bars! The package of 'voyage out, luxury hotel in Bermuda and voyage back' proved extremely popular. In addition, there were winter cruises to Cuba and elsewhere in the Caribbean.

At the end of the first year the newly formed Furness Bermuda Line bought the *Willochra* and *Wandilla* from the Adelaide Steamship Company and renamed them *Fort Victoria* and *Fort St George*. They also took over additional interests in hotels on the 'holiday isle' of Bermuda. The new ships, with a gross tonnage of 7,800, and which had been built in 1912, were larger and more comfortable than the old *Fort Hamilton*. Refitted with luxury accommodation for 380 first-class passengers and just fifty second-class passengers aft (set aside principally for the islanders), they proved extremely popular ships.

The *Fort Hamilton* (1903) was the founder member of the Furness Bermuda Line. (National Maritime Museum)

The *Fort St George* (1912) joined the Furness Bermuda Line in 1920.

The *Fort St George* suffered serious damage entering New York in March 1924, when the White Star Line's *Olympic* backed off her berth into the cruise ship. The collision was reportedly caused by the *Fort St George* racing the Royal Mail Steam Packet Company's *Arcadian* in from

Bermuda – the 'booze cruise ships' were seemingly under a curse. In his *History of the White Star Line*, Robin Gardner reports that:

> In the collision the *Fort St George*'s mainmast was snapped off at the base, 150 feet of decking was caved in, ventilators, rails, lifeboat davits were destroyed, the hydraulic derrick was badly mauled and the ship's radio antenna was brought down. In all the damage to the *Fort St George* was estimated at £35,000. It was believed at the time that the *Olympic* had escaped serious damage and so she proceeded with her voyage, but in reality the collision had broken her immense cast stern frame. Later repairs to the *Olympic* would involve replacing the entire frame, the first time such a repair had been undertaken with so enormous a vessel.

The elderly *Fort Hamilton* had to be retired in 1926 as too small and of inadequate standard for the trade on offer. Within a year the company commissioned a new purpose-built luxury liner, the *Bermuda*, with berths for 616 first-class passengers. The new ship was built by Workman Clarke at Belfast to exacting specifications, maximising passenger accommodation to a design that satisfied the shallow-draft requirements of Hamilton harbour. The result was a tall, beamy ship of 19,086 tons gross. She had four screws and four oil engines, slightly excessive but necessary if delays in service to her rich and demanding passengers were to be avoided. The engines were specially designed so that they did not protrude above D Deck, allowing full use of that level by passengers.

The first-class accommodation was equal to the finest on the Atlantic. The first-class passengers were provided for in well-appointed cabins, many with en-suite facilities, including six deluxe suites. Captain Isherwood reported in *Sea Breezes* that:

> She appeared in New York for the first time in January 1928, where her size and luxury on the Bermuda service caused a sensation. There was a Grand Social Hall, observation lounge, smoking room, library, gymnasium, Spanish style terrace café, and a 406-seater dining room. Fine open spaces were provided for games, promenade and dancing on the upper decks, much of that on A Deck being enclosed in glass. She immediately became so popular that off season cruises to the Caribbean were no longer necessary.

In 1929, one week before Christmas, the *Fort Victoria* was sunk following a collision near the Ambrose Light. Milton H. Watson described the loss in his book *Disasters at Sea*:

> At 4 o'clock the *Fort Victoria* came to a halt at the entrance to the Ambrose Channel. The moan of the sirens, the timed beat of melancholy bells and the sobbing blasts of whistle markers sounded on all sides. Suddenly, out of the grey clouds of fog, a tall sharp prow appeared. The [American] Clyde [Steamship Company's] liner, *Algonquin*, outbound for Galveston, cut a deep hole in the *Fort Victoria*, amidships on the port side. Both ships sent out an emergency signal, and police launches, Coast Guard vessels and tugs rushed to the scene. All passengers and crew from the *Fort Victoria* were quickly and safely evacuated, with Captain A.R. Francis being the last to leave. All were deposited safely in New York. At 7.30 p.m. the *Fort Victoria* slipped under the waves.

A second purpose-built ship was urgently needed on the Bermuda run and an order was placed with Vickers-Armstrong at Newcastle for an even larger vessel. Within only twelve months the ship was ready for launch and named *Monarch of Bermuda*. Only three months later disaster struck again when the *Bermuda* caught fire whilst waiting to embark passengers in Hamilton. The hulk

View from Paget, Bermuda.

The *Monarch of Bermuda* (1931) seen from Paget, Bermuda.

returned to her builders under her own power with the hope of eventually being returned back to service. Within three months she was stripped down to the upper deck ready for rebuilding, and only two months later the new decks and superstructure and even the funnels were in place. Then a second fire occurred, resulting in the total gutting of the ship and her sinking at Belfast. Later raised, the *Bermuda's* engines were salvaged and bought by the ship-builders, but the ship was wrecked off the coast of Sutherland whilst under tow to the breakers in the Forth.

Cunard Line's *Carinthia* was hastily chartered to help out. The *Carinthia* was succeeded by four return voyages of Canadian Pacific's *Duchess of Bedford* and a five-month charter of the *Franconia*. The subsequent arrival of the magnificent three-funnelled liner *Monarch of Bermuda* allowed the *Fort St George* to be disposed of. The *Monarch of Bermuda* was so successful on the route that a quasi-sister, the *Queen of Bermuda*, followed from Vickers the following year, this time from their yard at Barrow. She was the only large merchant-ship to be completed in 1932–33 (the *Queen Mary* was silent on the stocks on the Clyde at that stage of the Great Depression). The ships were registered at London under the ownership of the Furness Bermuda Line. Like the *Monarch of Bermuda*, manoeuvrability was enhanced by using turbo-electric drive with direct control from the bridge, coupled to four propellers – the day of the azimuth directional pod, let alone the bow thruster unit, was still a long way off. The *Queen of Bermuda* took her maiden departure from New York in February 1933. Despite the ending of Prohibition, the ships remained in demand by the high-class clientele, and over the next six years the pair remained a familiar sight at New York.

The *Monarch* and the *Queen* were essentially first-class luxury liners. The décor was a mixture of Art Deco and a gentleman's club, but there was a small second-class area aft, principally used by Bermudan residents. In contrast to other liners of this era, features such as the gymnasium and the swimming pool were prominent on A Deck and not hidden in the bowels of the ships, whereas

The *Queen of Bermuda* (1933) on trials before being handed over to her owners. Note that the funnels were then of equal height. (The Sankey Collection)

the children's nursery was concealed on the Promenade Deck between the funnels. The social focus at night was the A Deck dance hall, in which the orchestra was set centrally amidst dimmed coloured lights. The main lounge was two decks high, decorated in a honey colour with sycamore panelling and a tasteful sea-horse mural at one end; there was none of the pompously grand and heavy decoration seen on many of the contemporary North Atlantic liners.

The two ships maintained a twice-weekly departure from Piers 95–97 at New York, disembarking passengers into tenders at St George en route to the company hotels. The ships then proceeded to Hamilton to discharge up to 2,000 tons of drinking water, frozen goods and the occasional race horse or two. The voyage took only forty hours, but loading and unloading took up much of the remainder of the week.

Both ships spent the war trooping. In the immediate post-war refurbishment programme fire struck again, and the *Monarch of Bermuda* was declared a constructive total loss after being gutted at Belfast. She was towed away to the Fal to await her fate. With the shortage of ships at that time, she was taken over by the Ministry of Transport and rebuilt as the emigrant ship *New Australia*, later becoming the Greek Line's *Arkadia* before going to the scrap yard in 1966.

The *Queen of Bermuda* returned to service in February 1949 to provide a single ship service. Her three funnels were no longer the same height but stepped down from fore to aft. In time, her third dummy funnel was removed and in 1962 a new and rather ugly single funnel was installed along with new boilers, an air-conditioning plant and a new streamlined bow-section.

In 1951 the smaller *Ocean Monarch* was commissioned, from Vickers Armstrong, to run alongside the *Queen of Bermuda*. The *Ocean Monarch* had a passenger capacity of 438 first-class against the *Queen*'s post-war complement of 733. The *Ocean Monarch* was unique in that all the staterooms were on the outside, had adjoining bathrooms and many featured pullman-type beds which retracted into the bulkhead during the day to make a living room. The *Ocean Monarch* left

The *Ocean Monarch* (1951) was quite a contrast to her older consort, the *Queen of Bermuda*.

Barrow on her positioning voyage to New York via Tilbury in May 1951. There she was visited by the Lord Mayor of London, Alderman Denys Lowson, who gave her master, Captain L.F. Banyard, the gift of a silver enamelled cigar box to be presented to the Mayor of New York on arrival.

The *Ocean Monarch* ran a cruising programme to the Caribbean in the off-season, but the *Queen of Bermuda* remained on the Bermuda run. Marketing increasingly recognised that Bermuda was no longer the preserve of the very wealthy, and in the late 1950s a return fare to Bermuda started at only $153. The *Ocean Monarch* was given a flume stabilizer in 1963, when some additional cabins were also installed on the Promenade Deck. From then on both ships ran occasional cruises to the Caribbean and St Lawrence as trade fell away from the core service to Bermuda.

Competition from the air, increasing running costs, (particularly the price of fuel oil), plus increasingly stringent US Marine Safety Regulations, led inevitably to the withdrawal of the service in 1966. The *Ocean Monarch* was sold for further service. For a short while the post-war-built Cunard liner *Franconia* stepped into the breach to maintain the New York to Bermuda route, but alas this was short lived. In 1970 it was even reported that the Furness Group were negotiating with Vickers Limited at Barrow-in-Furness for a small cruise liner to maintain the Bermuda crossing in season and to be deployed elsewhere for the remainder of the year. However, no contract was ever placed.

The *Queen of Bermuda* was sold for scrap for just £225,000. Coincidentally she arrived at the breakers' yard in the same month that her sister, the Greek Line's cruise ship *Arkadia*, also went under the torch. Incredibly, the *Ocean Monarch* was destroyed by fire whilst refitting at Perama in 1981 under the ownership of World Cruise Lines, as the *Reina del Mar*. The curse of the 'booze-cruise ships' was unforgiving, with only the *Queen of Bermuda* and two of the three Forts managing to escape destruction by fire or loss at sea.

The C.T. Bowring & Company Red Cross Line also flourished during Prohibition, and in 1929 became part of the Furness group. The Red Cross Line maintained the elderly *Silvia* and

The *Nerissa* (1926) operated seasonal cruises to Bermuda for the Red Cross Line.

Rosalind and their flagship *Nerissa*, which was built at Port Glasgow in 1926, on a service from New York to St Johns with a seasonal extension to Bermuda. The *Nerissa* carried 230 passengers in two classes, but the accommodation was ordinary compared to that on the *Bermuda*. Under Furness ownership, the two older ships were replaced in 1936 by the sisters *Fort Amherst* and *Fort Townsend*, each with accommodation for 100 passengers. The trio continued to serve the route until the war, but passenger services were not resumed thereafter.

A number of other vessels cashed in on Prohibition and the need for a drink. When the Royal Mail Steam Packet Company's *Araguya* became a full-time cruise ship in 1924, she spent over half of the next six years taking thirsty Americans to Bermuda, Cuba or elsewhere in the Caribbean, and the summer season working from the UK. The *Avon* and *Arcadian* (ex-*Asturias*) were also used on the Bermuda run until Royal Mail withdrew from the service in 1930.

The Anchor Line's *Cameronia*, *Tuscania* and *Transylvania* were regulars in the New York cruise scene from 1921 until 1930, featuring mainly longer cruises to the Mediterranean, as well as helping to maintain the Cunard-Anchor joint transatlantic services. The first cruise was carried out by the *Cameronia* in November 1921 from New York to the Mediterranean. The following year the itinerary was extended to include Funchal, Monaco, Genoa, Naples and Bizerta. The *Transylvania* nearly came to grief on a cruise in March 1929 when she ran on to La Cocque rocks off Cherbourg. There was no panic amongst her American passengers although all had felt the impact. The boats were lowered to take depth soundings, and help was summoned, but she was able to back off the rocks and head to Cherbourg, listing and making water forward.

Even Cunard's mighty *Mauretania* was employed on winter cruises from New York to the Mediterranean from 1923 onwards. She was almost wholly dedicated to cruising in the 1930s (complete with obligatory white hull) until she was retired in 1934. Her first 'millionaires' cruise' left New York on 2 February 1923 and lasted a full six weeks to 7 April. One passenger paid $25,000

Anchor Line's *Transylvania* (1925) made a series of cruises out of New York between liner voyages.

for his suite for the voyage. In all, the *Mauretania* made a total of fifty-four cruises out of New York, either to the Mediterranean or the Caribbean. With 560 first-class and 475 second-class berths to fill, successful marketing was no mean achievement, although she typically only carried between 500 and 600 passengers on cruises, exceptionally 800 on the shorter 'booze cruises' out of New York. The elderly *Carmania* did a series of popular New York to Havana cruises in the late 1920s. The White Star Line was also involved and the brand new *Laurentic* ran two New York cruises to the Mediterranean during her first winter in service. In 1929 the *Majestic* and *Olympic* increased their takings by providing three-and-a-half-day return trips from New York to Halifax between liner voyages.

Canadian Pacific commissioned their four new Duchess-class liners in the late 1920s, just in time for the Depression. Three of them, the *Duchess of Atholl*, *Duchess of Richmond* and *Duchess of Bedford*, were engaged on short winter cruises to the Caribbean from New York in their early careers. Royal Mail Steam Packet's *Orbita* and *Orca* joined the fray in 1925, whereas their *Ohio* undertook an Italian charter, with pilgrims visiting the Vatican, on which access to alcohol might not have featured as highly as on other cruises out of New York!

The ultimate means of avoiding Prohibition was inaugurated in 1922 when the American Express Company chartered the Cunarder *Laconia* for a round-the-world cruise from New York. The 'Millionaires' cruise' carried 356 'tourists' to Japan, China, South Asia, the Middle East and Europe. Great play was made of the transit of the Panama Canal, when the Governor of the Panama Canal boarded at Cristobal with other local dignitaries and travelled to the Pedro Miguel Locks, where they disembarked. Senior members of the ship's crew were invited to join them in a tour of Bilbao, followed by dinner at the famous Tivoli House.

The American Express charter was clearly a success, and the *Samaria* repeated the route in 1923, followed by the *Franconia* in each of the three successive years. In 1923, however, there was competition from both the Canadian Pacific Line's *Empress of France* and the United American Line's *Resolute*. Most of these voyages were under charter to travel agencies, including Thomas Cook & Sons,

Raymond-Whitcomb Tour Company, Frank C. Clark and American Express. By 1926 the charterers had six ships involved, of which the British ones were the *Empress of Scotland*, the *Franconia*, *Laconia* and *Carinthia*. The first round-the-world cruise aimed at the cheaper end of the market was the charter by Frank C. Clark of the Anchor Line's *Caledonia* in 1927. Nevertheless the end was approaching, and as the Wall Street Crash attacked the disposable income in wealthy Americans' pockets, only one (foreign flag) ship did the round-the-world cruise in 1929.

At the other end of the market, the cheapest cruises lasted only a few hours before returning the inebriated cargo to New York. The Red Star Line's massive *Belgenland* was at the forefront of these booze cruises. She also undertook some longer cruises and at one time was the largest ship on the round-the-world voyages.

By 1933, as prices inevitably came down, the *New York Times* noted that it was possible to travel the globe for just $500, or 2 cents a mile. This could be accomplished by taking a series of second-class passages such as San Francisco-Yokohama-London-New York and overland by train back to San Francisco. Yet by 1933 there was no longer any need to go to sea for a drink – Prohibition had ended.

TYPES OF CRUISING

Author Donald Meek comments on the types of cruising that have been popular at one time or another, focussing on the social aspects rather than the normal economic pigeon-holing of 'millionaires' cruise', 'affordable' or 'mass-market cruise':

We are currently in a 'feely' age. It is also one which likes 'to get away from it all' while 'having it all' in a different dimension of existence. People can go to sea, and not want to see much anymore, as they concentrate on the shopping malls and restaurants. They do not really want to be part of the old 'natural world' – not on the big ships anyway. That is where the wee ships like the *Hebridean Princess* come in, they preserve the older, Edwardian model of cruising for the more visually aware, the people who like islands and some majestic rocks – and 'aspirational grandeur'. That is where small is beautiful (see Chapter 11).

There seem to be a number of different models of cruising: 'indulgence cruising' (the booze cruise), 'escapist cruising' (big ships, cut off from the larger world), 'sight seeing cruising' (the Edwardian ideal and the *Hebridean Princess* etc.), 'educational cruising' (British India Line etc.), reality cruising (*Dunara Castle* and *Hebrides*, banana boats, Booth Line, Elder Dempster Line, *St Helena* etc.).

The clever thing in all this is that in the modern world the cruise industry has succeeded in separating delight and pleasure from destination.

Realisation that service rather than destination was the key to selling most cruises became the salvation of many a liner suffering from decline in trade because of global economic recession or in later years when faced with stiff competition from the aeroplane. But this is a sad reflection of modern day social attitudes. How often have you heard the escapist cruise passenger recount to work colleagues and friends 'yes it was a wonderful cruise, the food was great, the entertainment marvellous…' rather than, 'what a wonderful sight the pyramids are and what an experience it was to traverse the Suez Canal'?

5

THE GREAT DEPRESSION

Dark tales were told of floating debaucheries and drunken orgies, but allowing for the invigorating sea air on human nature, the grade of decorum on board was probably no worse than that met in the licensed holiday hotel ashore. In fact the combined atmosphere of a crowded ship, in which the ubiquitous old ladies could give free rein to vigilance and gossip, might tend to keep behaviour within bounds. Possibly the sight of a cocktail bar shocked some who had hitherto never seen anything gayer than an aspidistra at the entrance to a dining room.

Keith P. Lewis, *Sea Breezes*, February 1950.

In August 1931 the pound fell from nearly $5 to $3.50 in value. Within months nearly a third of the British Merchant Navy was laid up with canvas-covered funnels, the ships lining the dock-sides, the Fal, the Thames estuary and the deep anchorages offered by numerous Scottish lochs. Thousands of seamen joined the ranks of the unemployed.

Overseas holidays were no longer tenable for British tourists, so the concept of travelling on a British cruise ship with fares bought in pounds and onboard currency also in pounds created a new industry. The industry was based on surplus tonnage and short duration cruises aimed at the mass market rather than the traditional luxury market. The Depression affected trade with North America the worst, and least affected trade with the Empire nations.

The lightly loaded North Atlantic liners were immediately available to start cruising, and the mighty *Mauretania* made the first five-day cruise for the Cunard Line with 836 passengers on a trip to Gibraltar in May 1932. She was followed into cruising by the *Aquitania*, also in May, and the *Berengaria* at the end of July, whilst the *Lancastria* commenced two-week cruises to the Mediterranean costing 21*s* per day. The *Lancastria* proved a popular cruising ship, and was briefly given an all-white hull in recognition of this. Several times she was chartered for special groups, including pilgrim organisations during Holy Year. Other ships in the fleet were maintained on the liner services; for example, the *Scythia* remained on the Liverpool to New York run with only a couple of cruises scheduled for her in the 1930s, whereas the *Laconia* and *Lancastria* were increasingly used for cruising as time went on. The *Franconia* and *Carinthia* continued their own cruise programme throughout the 1930s.

The cheap cruises offered by the *Berengaria* (1913) earned her the sobriquet 'The Bargain Area'.

The *Berengaria*'s first-class lounge.

The arrival of the new motor ships *Britannic* and *Georgic* displaced a number of ships to cruising in the White Star Line fleet. The *Britannic*'s accommodation was typical of the period style then in vogue, but the *Georgic* was given an altogether more modern décor and was by all accounts an extremely comfortable ship. In 1931 the *Adriatic* tried an experimental short weekend break cruise of two-and-a-half-days' duration over the August Bank Holiday, charging £5 for cabin accommodation and £3 for tourist. In 1932 the White Star Line operated fifteen short cruises and

The *Berengaria*'s first-class smoking room.

The ballroom aboard the *Berengaria*.

ten extended cruises using the *Olympic*, *Homeric*, *Calgaric* and *Adriatic* at peak holiday times and the *Doric* on full-time cruising. They were joined by the *Laurentic* on cruises to the Mediterranean from February onwards – a thirteen-day cruise cost just £15. The career of the *Doric* ended in 1935 following collision damage sustained off Vigo. The *Laurentic* had been laid down in 1920 but was only completed 'as cheaply as possible' some nine years later (there was, for example, a noticeable lack of carpeting in many of the public rooms); her twin reciprocating engines and

Swimming bath on the *Berengaria*.

The White Star Line's *Homeric* (1922) was scrapped at the age of fourteen. The cruising boom extended her career, but only for a short while.

single turbine affected her with a serious vibration problem. New York cruises were mainly operated by the *Olympic* and *Majestic*, and they were usually short trips to Bermuda or Halifax.

An editorial which first appeared in the December 1988 edition of *Sea Breezes* comments:

In our archives is a 1933 brochure advertising holiday cruises run by the White Star Line, then in the gathering dusk of its independent existence. It makes a contrast in promotional style from kindred

The Liverpool-based passenger tender *Skirmisher* (1884) was one of the more important units of the Cunard fleet. It was her job to service the liners in mid-river during their tight turnarounds between cruises.

literature of today. Only the cover, an artist's fantasy, is in colour, the pages within illustrated by black and white half-tone reproductions of photographs of places to be visited, and life on board. Most of the centre-spread is taken up with a montage of the five vessels forming 'The Cruising Fleet': *Adriatic, Calgaric, Doric, Homeric* and *Laurentic*.

It is noticeable at once that the average age of passengers, reflecting the socio-economic structure of the 1930s, appears to be younger than thirty-five. There is no sign of the twenties generation, so firmly targeted by the tour operators of the 1980s. Travellers are depicted enjoying traditional shipboard amusements, such as peg quoits, deck tennis, shuffleboard, tug-of-war and even a physical training class. Swimming had to be enjoyed in a rigged-up canvas pool, for of permanent cruising adjuncts there were none. The ships had been taken up from trade and the White Star directors sanguinely hoped that one day they might return to it.

None of the White Star cruise fleet was to return to trade. Three years after the publication of the brochure, four of them had been sold as scrap for the merged Cunard–White Star board. The surviving *Laurentic* enjoyed a trooping trip to troubled Palestine, a long lay-up, war service and then suffered three torpedoes from Kapitänleutnant Otto Kretschmer which ended her largely indeterminate career.

Cunard and White Star merged in 1934 in order to secure loans for the building of the *Britannic* and *Georgic* and to underwrite the order for the *Queen Mary*. Even the *Britannic* and *Georgic* were used on off-season cruises to the Caribbean, so desperate had trade become. The *Adriatic* was withdrawn and sold for scrap in 1934 for a paltry £48,000; the *Calgaric* went at the same time for £31,000, and the *Homeric* following in 1936 for £74,000. The *Olympic* and *Majestic* were also scrapped at that time. Between them they had carried 20,000 passengers, roughly 20 per cent

The *Melita* (1918) was a popular cruise ship in the Canadian Pacific fleet throughout the 1930s.

of the total cruise passengers carried from British ports, in just that first boom year of cheap cruises, 1932.

On Saturday 18 August 1935 over 600 passengers embarked for a Northern Capitals cruise aboard the *Laurentic* at Liverpool. Anchored in the Mersey in torrential rain whilst her passengers enjoyed a dance on the first evening aboard, she finally sailed in thick fog on the Sunday only to be rammed by the Blue Star Line's cargo ship *Napier Star*. The *Laurentic*'s crew accommodation was hit, and six men were killed outright and several others injured. Passengers were sent back to their cabins from muster stations in due course and returned to Liverpool on Monday morning to receive a full ticket refund. Although the damage included a 6-metre gash in the ship's side, she was repaired in time for a booked cruise in September with pilgrims from Dublin for Lourdes. On return she undertook one troop voyage and was laid up until the outbreak of war.

Canadian Pacific put the *Melita* on full-time cruising from July onwards, and she was soon joined by the *Montcalm*, *Montclare* and *Montrose*. The 'Monts' became full-time cruise ships for the remainder of the 1930s, offering twelve- to fourteen-day cheap cruises to Madeira, Teneriffe, Las Palmas and North Africa, and latterly also to Scandinavia out of London, Liverpool and Southampton. In all they made a total of 143 cruises from the UK before the outbreak of war in 1939. In the meantime, the larger Canadian Pacific Duchesses and Empresses tended to be used on longer and more expensive cruise programmes. Only the *Duchess of York* was exempt from cruising, whilst the other ships ran an extensive winter cruising programme from the UK and New York, as well as nine-day summer cruises from Montreal to New York and back. The *Duchess of Bedford*, for example, completed thirteen New York to the Caribbean cruises and four UK-based cruises in the 1930s, whilst the *Duchess of Richmond* carried veterans and their families to Gallipoli on a highly successful cruise in 1934.

Canadian Pacific's *Montrose* (1922) setting off on a cruise and dressed overall.

The *Empress of Australia*, completed as the German *Tirpitz* in 1919 but acquired by Canadian Pacific via the Repatriations Commission, was found to be an unsatisfactory unit until rebuilt and re-engined in 1926. Redesigned with an eye to winter cruising, she then became a most popular ship with the first of four round-the-world cruises taken in the winter of 1927–28, sharing the cruise market thereafter with the new *Empress of Britain*. From 1931 onwards she also undertook cruises to Norway and winter cruises out of New York to the Caribbean and the Mediterranean, as well as longer trips to southern Africa and South America. £8 bought a five-day cruise on the *Empress of Australia* to Corunna and Vigo, and 21 guineas bought fourteen days in Norwegian waters. The highlight for the *Empress of Australia* came in 1939 when she was chosen as the Royal Yacht to take King George VI across the Atlantic at the start of a tour of Canada and America.

Even the Donaldson Line resorted to some winter cruising, mainly to the Mediterranean, as relief from their fortnightly transatlantic sailings from Glasgow and Belfast. The service was maintained by the *Athenia* and her sister *Letitia* in collaboration with Cunard; the *Athenia* was ultimately destined to become the first casualty of the Second World War (see Chapter 7). They were big ships, with over 500 cabin-class berths and accommodation for 1,023 third-class passengers. They were, however, definitely not main-line ships as they had a service speed of only 15 knots.

The Belgian Red Star Line's British-registered *Belgenland* made a number of Mediterranean cruises in the early 1930s as a diversion from her normal transatlantic liner duties. Her apparent success as a cruise ship resulted in her sale to Panamanian interests in 1935 for use in the Caribbean. This venture was not profitable and the *Columbia*, as she had become, was scrapped the following year.

The Anchor Line's *Tuscania* started winter cruising, and cruising between voyages on the Bombay service. She made three cruises to the Mediterranean and one to Lisbon and Gibraltar from the UK in 1935, and three more to the Mediterranean the following year from Glasgow. Her final cruises were from Glasgow to the Western Isles in 1937, after which she was withdrawn and scrapped. The *Transylvania* was also used on cruising, making three twelve-day New York to Bermuda cruises in 1935; her Caribbean cruises peaked at a total of eight in 1938 and nine in 1939. These duties occupied her down time on the New York to Glasgow service. The *Caledonia* also undertook New York-based cruises to Bermuda and UK-based cruises to the Caribbean in the late 1930s.

Throughout the depressed years of the early 1930s the Royal Mail Steam Packet Company's *Atlantis* continued to return a profit for her owners. The once proud Royal Mail Company was all but bankrupt, only kept going by sleight of hand on the part of company chairman, Lord Kysant, who sanctioned a share issue with erroneous figures making the company look almost profitable. His philosophy of 'expand at times of depression because by the time the loans are called in the depression will be over', led him to sanction his recently acquired White Star Line to buy a minority interest in the Aberdeen & Commonwealth Line. The Great Depression, however, was deeper and longer than any before it.

The Royal Mail Steam Packet Company had been established by Royal Charter in 1838 to carry mail to the corners of the Empire. What a come down when the company chairman resigned in October 1931 and was subsequently tried and jailed for twelve months for his various acts of deception. The following year the Royal Mail Steam Packet Company was absorbed, along with the Nelson Line, David Maciver & Company and Royal Mail Meat Transports, into the newly incorporated Royal Mail Line. The *Atlantis* cruised through all the furore undeterred, bringing pleasure to countless passengers on extensive long-distance cruises, short Norwegian cruises and long weekend breaks.

There were a number of other liners-cum-cruise ships which were highly successful, and one of these came about for the wrong reasons. The sinking of the Lamport & Holt liner *Vestris*, dating from 1911, following a routine departure from New York to Buenos Aires via Brasil in 1929 with the loss of 112 lives, caused the company to withdraw from the New York passenger service altogether. The demise of the Lamport & Holt Line allowed Furness Withy to step into the breach. Four remarkably luxurious passenger cargo liners were immediately ordered by their subsidiary company, the Prince Line. These were the Compass Princes: *Northern Prince*, *Eastern Prince*, *Southern Prince* and *Western Prince*. The four-ship service was up and running by early 1930, renewing British interests on the New York to River Plate route. It also gave Americans another cruise opportunity.

With the downfall of Lord Kylsant's Royal Mail Group, subsidiary company Lamport & Holt was placed in the hands of the receiver and the future looked bleak. The sisters *Vandyck* and *Voltaire*, dating from 1922 and 1923 respectively, were duly taken out of service and laid up. As built, the *Vandyck* could accommodate 309 first-class, 144 second and 222 third-class passengers, and the *Voltaire* 278 first, 134 second and 212 in third class. The public rooms included a particularly fine first-class lounge, a music room, smoke room and veranda café. There was also a gymnasium and a children's playroom. The second class had a lounge and smoke room. Heating was by steam radiators and ventilation was provided by large air ducts under forced draft with electric fans in all rooms.

In August 1932 the rising interest in cruising to the sun saw the *Voltaire* refitted as a full-time cruise ship, featuring outside cabins for all passengers, two swimming pools and a shop operated by John Lewis, their first venture to sea. So successful was the cruise ship *Voltaire* that the *Vandyck* was also reactivated and converted ready for her inaugural cruise out of Liverpool in June 1933, just ten-and-a-half months after her sister's cruise debut. In 1937 both ships received major refits in which their conversion from passenger liner to cruise ship became irreversible. Sadly both ships

The Lamport & Holt liner *Voltaire* (1923), resplendent in cruising white livery, at anchor whilst her passengers are ashore.

came to violent ends in the war, the *Voltaire* as an armed merchant cruiser and the *Vandyck* as an armed boarding vessel.

P&O had operated luxury off-season cruises since the late 1920s, but joined the short cruise market using the *Moldavia* and *Mongolia*. These were tourist-class ships used on the emigrant service to Australia and provided ideal UK summer cruise ships for the mass market. There were one or two minor incidents: a collision in July 1933 between the *Mongolia*, the breakwater and a tanker in Copenhagen after the liner had lost her anchor, and an engine breakdown aboard the Mongolia in the Mediterranean in July 1935.

The luxury end of the market continued to be supported by P&O, with the *Viceroy of India* running summer Scandinavian and Mediterranean cruises since the 1929 season, whilst carrying the mails out to India in the winter. She even operated winter extension cruises from Bombay on to Bali. The cruise season was intensive; for example, in 1933 the *Viceroy of India* left London as follows:

12 May for Greece and Egypt;
10 June for Spain, Portugal and Monte Carlo;
14 July for Casablanca, Las Palmas, Madeira and Teneriffe;
29 July to the Northern capitals;
19 August for Algiers, Italy and Spain.

Amongst other P&O liners used for summer cruises to the Baltic, Adriatic and the Mediterranean were the popular 'white sisters' *Strathaird* and *Strathnaver*. Both ships survived the war to be scrapped in the early 1960s. In addition the Indian R-class steamers *Rajputana*, *Ranchi*, *Ranpura* and *Rawalpindi* operated low-season cruises from the UK to the Mediterranean.

The traditional baronial hall, country house hotel-style incorporated in the first-class smoking room aboard the *Viceroy of India* (1929). (DP World)

The new *Strathnaver* (1931) is pulled away from the fitting out quay at Barrow to make room for the *Strathaird* (1932). (The Sankey Collection)

The *Orford* (1928) lies at anchor in a Norwegian fjord awaiting the return of her cruise passengers.

The Orient Line was also active from the late summer of 1933 onwards, with two-week cruises to the Mediterranean and Scandinavia by the *Orontes*, *Orford*, *Orama* and *Ormonde*, and two longer cruises by the *Orford*. In addition the *Otranto* inaugurated a call at Majorca for holiday makers to visit the island and await the next Orient Line ship homeward bound from Australia.

The brand-new *Orcades* was an improved version of the *Orion* and near sister of P&O's *Strathallan*. She carried out a shakedown cruise from Tilbury via Southampton to the Mediterranean on delivery in August 1937, much as the *Orion* had in 1935, before assuming liner duties to the Antipodes. Sadly, this ultra-modern and popular vessel, affectionately known to the Australians as 'The Big Tug', was lost in the war, although her near sister, the *Orion*, survived in service into the 1960s. The initial schedule for the *Orion* included two return trips to Australia during the winter months and a summer season spent cruising as a first-class-only vessel. The summer cruises included a Southampton departure to the Mediterranean and several North European cruises based on the port of Immingham. The *Orcades* also undertook some seasonal cruises.

One memorable feature of these ships is that their interiors were designed by the young architect Brian O'Rorke, and were founded on light and space, rather than the traditional heavy furnishings of the country house hotel style which was previously favoured. The *Orion* and *Orcades* were the first British liners to feature part air-conditioning, and the first to have fire alarm and sprinkler systems. Passenger suggestions on cabin design were incorporated such that doors could be left open in hot weather, beds could be stowed away in the day, and flasks of iced water made available.

P&O first tested the Australian cruise market with the *Strathaird* and Orient Line with the *Oronsay*, both in 1932. A landmark was the introduction of Orient Cruises between Australia and New Zealand in 1935, which at last put cruising firmly on to the Australian market.

Meanwhile the luxury cruises maintained by ships such as the *Arandora Star* and the *Atlantis* continued to be well patronised. Destinations included Africa and the Caribbean as well as more typical venues such as the Mediterranean, Madeira and Las Palmas.

'The Big Tug' *Orcades* (1937) was built for off-season cruising, but sadly was lost in the war.

In 1933, 170,000 cruise passengers sailed out of UK ports (the figure was just over 1 million in 2004). UK-flagged vessels also serviced the demand for cruising out of the United States; the *Mauretania* was despatched to New York after only three UK-based cruises, where she carried out a further fifty-one dollar-earning cruises until she was retired in 1935.

Even the Blue Funnel Line had to resort to cruising. The Government had previously persuaded the company to offer a passenger service on their fast UK to Brisbane cargo route via the Cape. In response, the sisters *Aeneas*, *Ascanias* and *Anchises* were commissioned in 1910 and 1911, followed by the slightly larger *Nestor* and *Ulysses* in 1913. The original trio offered 283 first-class-only berths but this was reduced to 180 after the First World War. In the early 1920s Blue Funnel brought out the *Sarpedon* followed by the *Patroclus*, *Hector* and *Antenor* for the Far Eastern services, but unlike the Australian ships the Far Eastern ships were never used to attract tourist traffic. The ships were cosy and informal, and a classic feature was that the dining saloon stretched across the full width of the ship.

The *Nestor* and the *Ulysses*, ships graced by the world's tallest single funnels, carried 350 passengers in first class, but this was reduced to just 175 in the mid-1930s. Promotional literature describes them as 'without any magnificence but with the good solid comfort which is essential to the enjoyment of a long voyage'. Before the passenger accommodation was reduced, the *Nestor* and *Ulysses* offered a number of four-month return-trips to Brisbane, complete with a trip to the Great Barrier Reef, all for £135. This was a popular voyage for British passengers, as well as South Africans who elected to return home from Britain 'the long way round'. The company brochure read:

> *Ulysses* is not a cruising vessel in the generally accepted sense as she will be about her lawful occasions, carrying cargo to the various ports of call in the Straits and Java, and from the main ports of Australia and South Africa … but ample time will be allowed at each for passengers to visit the scenes of beauty and of interest inshore.

The *Anchises* (1911) carried first-class round-trip passengers in two, three and four-berth cabins to Australia via the Cape.

A Union-Castle ship coaling at the Bluff in Durban.

A contemporary account of one of the voyages describes visits to the stoke-hold and its seventy Chinese stokers, a masked ball in a temperature of 40°C to which the best costume prize was given to a wearer of a loin cloth, and visits to the Temple of Snakes in Sumatra. Passengers were allowed ashore on Piper Island off the Australian coast, where they were encouraged to collect pieces of coral and large shells. The Chinese stokers boiled the contents of the shells for their tea, returning the cleaned shells to the passengers. The account also describes coaling at the Bluff, Durban, where teams of men shovelled coal into large scoops which were lifted by crane and emptied into the ship's bunkers at the pull of a rope accompanied by clouds of coal dust. Leonard Pendlebury, a junior officer, describes the scene in an article which first appeared in *Sea Breezes* in June 1949:

> The Boat Deck was covered to a depth of several inches in coal dust. It was a thoroughly miserable experience, and I recall that I used up four white suits in the three days we were alongside at the Bluff.

Both the *Nestor* and *Ulysses* were later used for seasonal summer cruising to the Baltic and Poland, the *Nestor* being so employed at the outbreak of war in September 1939. Considering the massive chilled cargo space aboard these vessels, this was desperate employment indeed.

The Glasgow-based Paddy Henderson passenger and cargo service to Burmah via Suez was maintained in the 1920s and 1930s by the *Pegu*, *Kemmendine* and *Amarapoora*. Dorothy Laird in her history of the company reports:

> Henderson ships also joined in the great contemporary enthusiasm for cruises of all kinds and short holiday trips between the UK and the Continent were arranged with their passenger vessels, which were used as hotels by the passengers during their stay in Continental ports. These trips which lasted seven or eight days and cost about £1 per day – in some cases including the railway ticket to the port of embarkation – proved understandably popular.

In 1932, in a bid to fill berths on the New Zealand service from the UK, the Shaw Savill Line introduced an all-inclusive round cruise ticket for just £111. This was inaugurated by the *Akaroa* and followed by her running-mates, the *Mataroa* and *Tamaroa*, all three being former Aberdeen Line ships. The inclusive fare provided bed and board for nearly three months, the return trip to New Zealand plus the trip round the New Zealand coast between ports. The three-ship service was a huge success for the remainder of the 1930s, with revenue boosted by the cruise passengers.

Other cruise ventures were nearer to home. In 1932 the Wilson Line placed their elderly *Calypso* on round voyages from Hull and London to Danish and Norwegian ports, offering her seventy-six first-class berths on a cruise basis whilst the ship went about its normal business. These were so successful that by the summer of 1934 the associate Ellerman City Line had to take the *City of Paris* off their Indian service to satisfy demand. The cruises were repeated annually until the *City of Nagpur* was placed on the summer cruise circuit from 1936 onwards. In the meantime the *Calypso*, which had started her days running between Belgium and the Congo as the *Bruxllesville* in 1897, had been sold for scrap. Throughout the 1930s the Ellerman & Bucknall Line offered their sixty-five-day round trip to South African ports, first-class only, for a fare of 80 guineas.

Some of the big passenger liners completed in this era were designed with an eye to off-season 'yachting cruises' (see Chapter 3). Ships such as P&O's *Viceroy of India*, the brand new sisters *Strathnaver* and *Strathaird* and the Orient Line's *Orcades* and *Orion* were good examples, and Canadian Pacific's *Empress of Britain* was also specially equipped for winter cruises. Other ships were converted permanently for cruising, such as the former Royal Mail Steam

The *Tamaroa* (1922) was built as the Aberdeen line's *Sophocles*. Under Shaw Savill ownership she offered round-trip cruises to New Zealand as part of her liner duties.

Packet/Pacific Steam Navigation Company passenger liner *Andes*, built in 1913 for service between Southampton, Buenos Aires and Montevideo. She had become the cruise ship *Atlantis* in 1929, a role in which she excelled throughout the Depression. So also did the famous Blue Star Line luxury cruise ship *Arandora Star*, one of the first ships to offer short cruises with one-day taster cruises from Bournemouth in May 1931, designed to draw the English middle classes to cruising.

The Pacific Steam Navigation Company supplemented its services in 1931 with a Welsh-speaking cruise to Norway by the *Orduna*. This was such a success that a second cruise was arranged soon afterwards, this time to Morocco. The *Orbita* was also used for cruising between liner voyages. The *Reina del Pacifico* undertook a shakedown cruise when she was commissioned in 1931, but thereafter remained on liner duties to the west coast of South America.

Many other liners were fitted out for cruising on a temporary or seasonal basis in the 1930s. An account by Frank Bowen, published in 1938 (see references), describes the seasonal conversion of passenger liners into cruise ships as follows:

> Very little has to be done to the ordinary mail steamer to fit her for a cruising yacht. As a rule her maximum passenger accommodation is very much smaller than when she is on her regular service, in order to provide greater comfort, while some re-arrangement of the furniture in the public rooms may be necessary to give opportunities of amusement if the weather makes the decks uncomfortable. Being without cargo she is liable to be lively in any sea, which is the last thing that the cruising passenger desires, so that all her water ballast tanks are filled as a matter of course, and as a rule she takes on board a certain amount of extra solid ballast, distributed in such a way that her motion is made as easy as possible. Sometimes it is necessary to give her extra motor boats for the convenience of passengers landing for shore excursions, but many ships are already sufficiently equipped in that direction.

HMT *Neuralia* (1912) inaugurated the British India Line's school cruise programme in 1932.

The Depression encouraged companies such as the Union-Castle Line and P&O to offer cruises along the South African and Australian coasts on the normal services of their mail ships. These remained popular well into the 1970s when the liner services finally ceased altogether. Union-Castle Line's around-Africa service remainder popular until the last.

The 1930s cruise boom had all but run its course by 1935. Even so, 250 UK-based cruises had been provided in 1934. Not only was the *Mauretania* withdrawn, but so too were the *Doric* and *Laurentic*, both involved in collisions whilst cruising and considered unfit for repair. The length of the depressed years was just too long, and the profit margin on mass-market cruising too small. The Annual Report for the Orient Line in 1935 states:

> We dispatched four ships on sixteen cruises and although we earned more than the running cost
> of the ships it was not enough to pay for their depreciation. The cruises are always conducted on a
> narrow margin of profit.

Notwithstanding, cruising remained an important source of employment for many ships, allowing them continued employment until the outbreak of war in 1939. So popular had cruising become that Whitbread advertised their Pale Ale under the slogan 'Ten Thousand Bottles Per Cruise', and Selfridges introduced their 1936 swimwear collection against a backdrop of the swimming pool aboard the *Atlantis*.

THE STUDENT CRUISE MARKET

On 26 March 1932 Canadian Pacific Line's *Montrose* sailed for Casablanca with 750 school children from forty-five different schools. She was joined by White Star Line's *Doric* on 28 March, which set off with 900 school children and 400 parents to Ceuta. There were three cruises in 1933 operated by the *Doric* and *Montcalm*, and the *Doric* and *Adriatic* were used the following year. The *Adriatic*, *Calgaric* and *Laurentic* undertook a number of charters for 'Guiders and Scouters', at least one of which included the Chief Scout, Lord Baden-Powell, and his wife in the 650-strong passenger list on a Baltic cruise.

In 1932 British India Line inaugurated their schools programme with the sailing of the troopship *Neuralia* from Leith on 25 July to Scandinavian and Baltic ports, and in the summers between 1935 to 1937 she was joined by sister ship *Nevasa*. They had originally been built for the UK to Calcutta service in 1912 and 1913 respectively. There was also a programme of cheap cruises for parties of schoolboys which commenced in 1935. The boys were accommodated on the troop decks with supervisors in the available cabins. With the arrival of the new troopships *Dilwara* and *Dunera* in 1936 and 1937, the seasonal cruises were run using the new ships outside the trooping season. The cruises were again targeted at boys, all of whom were berthed in the troop quarters, with parents, teachers and other adults occupying the passenger cabins.

The *Dilwara* and *Dunera* were the first purpose-built troopships to be ordered for many years. As such they set new pre-war standards for the carriage of troops and their families. A condition of the design was that they could both operate on conventional British India commercial services if required, but, as troop transports with no cargo being carried, 2,500 tons of road metal acted as permanent ballast in numbers 1 to 4 and number 7 holds. The passenger accommodation was completed to a very high standard, with the conventional first-class music room, smoking room and café/lounge on the Promenade Deck. The first-class area was in strong contrast to the austerity of the troop decks, with their portable tables and hammock hooks. The full complement of these ships was:

Commissioned Officers 104 first class

Warrant Officers 100 second class

Troop families 164 family accommodation

Troops 1,154 main and lower decks

Crew 209

Total: 1,731 men and women

The troop accommodation was sparse and consisted of hammocks slung at night over daytime mess tables, although this arrangement was replaced by bunks after the war. On the lower deck was 'a detention room for disciplinary purposes', and young off-season cruise passengers would have this pointed out to them as warning of misbehaviour! There were extensive medical and hospital areas including a padded cell and a mental ward. The only recreational facilities appear to have been a writing room. The elderly *Neuralia* was lost in the war and the *Nevasa* was broken up in 1948, but the *Dilwara* and *Dunera* continued after the war, the latter becoming the nucleus of a new schools programme which started in 1961 (see Chapter 8).

6

BUTTERFLIES, COASTAL LINERS AND CRUISE FERRIES

But with the coming of another war, the paddle steamers once again turned to trooping; some with great success. The *Royal Eagle*, for instance, survived 43 dive bomb attacks. Though when that war ended the butterfly boats gradually died out, until in the 1950s they became strange antiques in an age of motorways and electric railways.

From an article by Norman Fox which first appeared in *The Illustrated London News*,

23 January 1971.

Day trips were widely available by paddle steamer, 'weather and other circumstances permitting'. The steamers plied the Thames, Clyde, Bristol Channel and the Forth, and worked from an array of other centres including all the main seaside resorts that offered a suitable pier or quay for the vessels to berth. The so-called 'butterfly boats' (which came out in the summer and flitted about) had developed a following which peaked in 1914, and whose post-First World War revival was inhibited by the arrival of the motor coach. Some of the longer routes spawned crack turbine steamers, but these were not always suitable for pier-hopping as their heavy gear-trains did not allow fast stops and starts.

Although the popularity of the paddle steamer waned through the 1920s and 1930s, a number of new vessels were commissioned. Typical of the very large paddle steamer was the General Steam Navigation Company's *Royal Eagle*, which at 1,539 tons gross and a capacity to carry 2,000 day passengers, dwarfed some of the earlier vessels operating on the Thames. She was completed in time for the 1932 season and operated mainly on the Tower Bridge to Southend, Margate and Ramsgate service. She required a crew of thirty plus seventy catering staff, and could seat 310 at one sitting in the dining saloon. The largest excursion paddle steamer of all was the *La Marguerite*, built in 1894 for Palace Steamers and operated by the Victoria Steamboat Association on day-trips from Tilbury to Margate and Boulogne, before transferring to the Liverpool & North Wales Steamship Company in 1904. That company's souvenir guide described *La Marguerite* as 'a swagger ship and the finest paddle steamer ever built for pleasure'.

The last 'butterfly boats' were built just after the Second World War. They were the *Cardiff Queen* and *Bristol Queen* for P&A Campbell on the Bristol Channel, and the *Waverley* for the Craigendoran-based Clyde routes of the London & North Eastern Railway. The *Waverley* alone

Contrast the apparent luxury of the Barry Railway Company's *Devonia* (1905) seen off Penarth in an Edwardian summer with...

...the austere wooden-hulled *Queen of the North* (1895) which ran pleasure cruises from Blackpool as far afield as Douglas throughout the Edwardian summers.

The New Medway Steam Packet Company's day excursion vessel *Queen of the Channel* (1935) emulated the style of the big cruise ships such as the *Arandora Star*. This company postcard has smoke dubbed in from both funnels, the forward one being a dummy funnel!

remains in service today, operating seasonally from a variety of areas around the UK and marketed as the last sea-going paddle steamer. She remains very popular, but depends on charitable contributions for maintenance. Now over sixty years old, her continued operation is no mean feat.

An interesting spin-off from the butterfly boat was the motor excursion ship. Many sported twin funnels, and most had cruising white hulls and looked like miniature versions of the *Arandora Star*. Typical of this type of vessel were the *Royal Lady* and *Coronia* at Scarborough, the *St Silio* at Liverpool and the *Queen of the Channel*, built in 1935 for the New Medway Steam Packet Company for service on the Thames. The *Queen of the Channel* was the first of a series of similar ships, which came from William Denny's yard at Dumbarton. The *Queen of the Channel* was only marginally smaller than General Steam's paddler *Royal Eagle*. The General Steam Navigation Company recognised the threat of the new motor 'steamer', and promptly bought out the New Medway Steam Packet Company, although the New Medway Company was allowed to retain its own identity.

In the Second World War many of the paddle steamers and small motor excursion boats went to the beaches at Dunkirk whilst others were converted for coastal defence work. Dunkirk survivors include the *Princess Elizabeth*, an Isle of Wight paddle ferry, now appropriately moored in Dunkirk harbour, whilst the *Coronia* and *Regal Lady* are still in service running seasonal excursions out of Scarborough.

A popular alternative to rail travel was to take time out and relax aboard the coastal liner. The coastal voyages offered a few days at sea on passage between London and Glasgow, Dublin, Liverpool, Newcastle, Leith, Dundee or Aberdeen. After the First World War some services were revived but the coastal liner was in decline and the cruise element of the first-class clientele was finally eroded by the onset of the Great Depression. Although some services continued through

Coast Lines' *Southern Coast* (1911) maintained the Liverpool to London coastal liner route – a two-week round trip with accommodation for eighty passengers.

the 1920s and 1930s, none survived after the Second World War, save for the twelve passenger cargo ships of Coast Lines Limited, which maintained the Liverpool to London route until 1967.

The coastal liner had comfortable accommodation for first-class passengers with slightly more austere second-class facilities. Trading between her home port and London, there might be intermediate calls at ports such as Plymouth out and Falmouth return, plus Southampton and Dublin on the run between Liverpool and London. For many years the London to Liverpool service was provided by the Coast Lines' steamer *Southern Coast*, built originally for Hough Line as the *Dorothy Hough* in 1911. She could carry eighty passengers and sailed on a two-week round trip, loading and unloading cargo as required.

Other passenger-carrying steamers on the west coast were operated by the British & Irish Steam Packet Company. The route was at its most popular just before the First World War when there were four sailings per week in each direction. The ships could complete the voyage from Dublin to London, with intermediate stops at a variety of ports, in four days at a speed of 13 knots. They had accommodation for 120 saloon and fifty second-class passengers. The route was advertised under the Edwardian banner 'Grand Summer Cruises', and single fares were 27s 6d saloon and 19s 6d second class. Food was not included but passengers could either pay for each individual meal or buy a contract ticket for all meals at 23s 0d saloon or 17s 0d second class. Guinness stout was available at 4d a bottle and a basin of soup cost 4d, the soup available only to second-class passengers.

The last steamers to be built for the Dublin to London service were the *Lady Wimborne* and the *Lady Cloé*, both in 1915. They had accommodation for seventy first-class passengers only, and at the end of the First World War resumed the passenger service with intermediate calls at Cork, Falmouth, Torquay and Southampton against a £5 single passage ticket. The passenger service ceased in 1933.

William Sloan & Company carried passengers on their Glasgow–Belfast–Bristol route until 1932, when it became cargo only. The Clyde Shipping Company had a daily departure from Springfield Quay at Glasgow for London, Southampton, Belfast, Dublin or Waterford from the 1900s. In the 1930s the round-trip fare was 60s 0d, meals extra, for a Glasgow to Dublin, Waterford and Cork voyage lasting five days. The ships had open bridges until the Second World War, and it is said that the Deck Officers were easily recognised ashore by their weather-beaten appearance!

The 1939 Clyde Shipping Company timetable offered the following inclusive first-class round-trip fares from Glasgow: a seven-day trip to Belfast, Waterford and Plymouth, £4 5s 0d; nine-day trip to Belfast and London, £5 5s 0d; and a six-day trip to Dublin, Waterford and Cork for £3 5s 0d. Similar fares were offered for a variety of round-trips from London, changing ship for the return voyage. An attractive round trip was offered for £4 10s 0d, north to Glasgow, by a Clyde Shipping Company steamer on Tuesday from London. The return was from Dundee on Wednesdays by Dundee, Perth and London Shipping Company vessel, arriving at London on Friday some thirty-four hours later, or from Leith by London & Edinburgh Shipping Company steamer on Monday, Wednesday or Saturday. The same timetable advised that breakfast was served at 8.30 a.m., dinner at 1 p.m. and tea at 6.30 p.m. A bottle of beer cost 9d and a whisky was 1s 8d; champagne, it appears, was sold by the pint bottle at 10s 6d a time.

The steamers of the Dundee, Perth and London Shipping Company used to call twice-weekly at Southend Pier to collect and disembark passengers on the thirty-hour run north, so saving the additional four-hour journey up to Limehouse. The London & Edinburgh Shipping Company, operating to Leith, maintained the 1924-built *Royal Fusilier* and the 1928-built *Royal Archer*, of 2,187 and 2,266 tons gross respectively. These were popular ships in summertime on the east coast; they could carry 116 passengers in first-class cabins and 130 in second-class in four-, six- and eight-berth cabins. At peak times additional accommodation was offered in a ten-berth dormitory and in the public spaces. Both ships were lost in the early years of the war and the East Coast passenger service finally ceased.

Aberdeen also had a direct connection to London maintained by the Aberdeen Steam Navigation Company. The Newcastle to London route was maintained by the Tyne-Tees Steam Shipping Company, with the *Hadrian* and the *Bernicia* built in 1923 by the Hawthorn Leslie & Company and Swan Hunter & Wigham Richardson respectively. They were not sisters in that the *Bernicia* had a gross tonnage of 1,936 and accommodation for 136 first-class passengers amidships and 100 second-class in dormitory accommodation aft, while the *Hadrian* could carry 176 first- and 508 second-class passengers. The single fare for the twenty-four-hour journey from the Tyne to London was 12s 6d including berth and food.

Cruises were also available on some coastal steamers. M. Langlands & Sons had pioneered cruising to the Western Isles of Scotland. The company was absorbed into the Coast Lines group after the First World War and with it came the role of providing Scottish cruises. For this purpose the Burns & Laird ferry *Tiger*, which was normally employed on the Glasgow to Dublin ferry service, operated cruises out of Liverpool in 1922 and 1923 but was replaced by the newly built *Lady Louth* in July. The *Lady Louth* was built for the Liverpool to Dublin overnight service, but could not initially take up station due to a strike. Between 1924 and 1926 the cruises were again offered by the *Tiger* but on a restricted summer season, as she could not be released from ferry duties during the Glasgow holiday period in July each year.

In 1927 the cruise season became the province of the 'cruising yacht' *Killarney* owned by the City of Cork Steam Packet Company, and transferred to Coast Lines' ownership in 1931.

The *Killarney* (1893) was built for the Belfast to Liverpool overnight ferry service but was fitted out as a dedicated cruise ship in 1927.

The *Killarney* had been built in 1893 by Harland & Wolff as the *Magic* and later renamed the *Classic*, was given yellow funnels and a grey hull and put on the cruise roster out of Liverpool. Based at Liverpool, she called either at Belfast or Ardrossan to pick up additional passengers for the West Highland cruises. The *Killarney* also offered start and end of season round-Britain cruises. She survived the Second World War but was deemed unfit to return to civilian duties and was sold in 1947.

During the 1930s, the Belfast Steamship Company's *Ulster Prince* and *Ulster Queen* undertook a series of weekend cruises, starting on Saturday mornings, to the Scottish Isles. On the final cruise in 1939, the *Ulster Prince* temporarily grounded on Rathlin Island. Cruises were also offered to the Channel Islands by the Cork to Fishguard ferry *Innisfallen* out of Cork in 1934.

The post-Second World War replacement for the *Killarney* was another former British & Irish Steam Packet Company ferry, the 3,222 gross ton *Lady Killarney*. She dated from 1912 and had carried the names *Lady Connaught*, *Lady Leinster* and *Patriotic* before adopting her cruising role. She too was given the buff-coloured hull and yellow funnel of the cruise liner, and placed under the command of her wartime captain, Peter Mullan. The light-coloured hull proved to be an impracticality and became green after only three seasons, but in 1952 it reverted to the black and white livery of Coast Lines. As the *Lady Connaught*, a wartime hospital ship, much of her fittings had been stripped out and the job of reconstructing her as a luxury cruise vessel was considerable. Nonetheless this was done, and she emerged complete with a 100-seat restaurant on the main deck, a spacious entrance area combining the staircases to the main and Promenade Decks, a card room on the lower deck and a timbered smoke room on the boat deck. The old ship survived on her seasonal roster until withdrawn, much to the anguish of her regular clientele, in 1956.

It was planned to use the relatively new *Irish Coast* (delivered in 1952) on the West Highland cruise programme in 1957. Alas, this was foiled by the delayed availability of a sister ship covering for refits and, even though adverts picturing the vessel in a Scottish loch appeared in *Punch* and other

The LNER ferry *Vienna* (1930) ran a series of successful cruises.

journals, the cruises never took place. However, the story does not end there. In 1989 the Caledonian MacBrayne car and passenger ferry *Columba* was bought by Leisure & Marine Holdings and placed on a seasonal West Highland cruising roster based at Oban under the name *Hebridean Princess*. Built originally with a passenger complement of 600, she was totally redesigned on the country house hotel principle with exclusive accommodation for just forty-nine 'guests' and a crew of thirty-five. A seven-day cruise typically ranged in price between £1,000 and £3,000 (see Chapter 11).

Cruises by railway-owned ships were first undertaken in the 1920s. The 1924-built *St Briac* from Southern Railway's Southampton to St Malo service commenced a series of four-day cruises in 1932. These took in destinations such as Le Havre, Rouen, Jersey, Guernsey, St Malo and Antwerp. She carried only 165 passengers on these trips and even sported a temporary open-air swimming pool. The cruises continued throughout the 1930s; there were fifteen of them in 1932, twenty-two in 1933 and a further nineteen in 1934.

The London & North Eastern Railway also undertook spring and summer weekend cruises to Holland from 1932 onwards, using the turbine steamer *Vienna*. These were always extremely popular and included tours of the bulb fields, using the ship as a hotel, and weekend cruises to other ports including Antwerp, Ghent and Zeebrugge. The lounge accommodation aboard the *Vienna* was increased in 1936 in recognition of her cruising role. The earliest cruises appear to have been the positioning voyages between winter service in the Irish Sea and summer duties at Hull by the London & North Eastern Railway's *Duke of Clarence* and her successor the *Duke of Connaught*. These took place between 1926 and 1932, either via Scotland or Jersey, and the cruises were extremely popular.

Post-war cruises were offered initially by the Southampton based steamer *Falaise*. These were usually summer-weekend cruises to St Malo, Jersey or Rouen, but she also operated some cruises from Folkestone to the Netherlands during the tulip season. Her first cruise took place in summer 1948.

The ornate first-class smoking room aboard the *Vienna*.

The *Duke of Lancaster* was one of three similar ships introduced onto the overnight Heysham to Belfast ferry service in 1956, and part of her role was to carry on the cruising tradition started in the 1930s. She was a twin-screw turbine steamer with a gross tonnage of 4,797. Her interior decoration included some varnished woodwork, but widespread use was also made of plastic veneers. She normally accommodated 1,500 passengers in two classes, but her cruise ship accommodation was single-class only and greatly reduced in numbers; several of her cabins were modified to provide additional bathroom facilities for cruise passengers.

The *Duke of Lancaster*'s cruises took place at the start and end of the summer season, to destinations in the West Highlands and Islands and to the continent, as far south as Portugal and north as Norway and Denmark. Cruises normally started from Heysham, but some started at Harwich and some at Plymouth. The West Highland cruises commenced in 1958, when it was clear that Coast Lines could no longer fulfil this role. Whilst on Western Isles cruises, however, she normally took the Belfast Steamship Company's Captain J.B. Wright with her to act as pilot – he had been the last captain of Coast Lines' *Lady Killarney*. On these cruises two of the ship's boats were used as tenders with their sterns heavily ballasted with rocks collected from the shore, in order to keep the propellers submerged when returning empty from shore or ship. The *Duke of Lancaster* carried out her final cruise in 1966.

The last of the railway ferries to be designed for, and engaged to any extent in, cruising was the Harwich-based conventional ferry the *Avalon*. She was launched without ceremony on 7 May 1963 from Alexander Stephen & Sons' yard on the Clyde. She was a large ship for her day and had a gross tonnage of 6,584, and could accommodate 750 passengers in two classes, with cabin berths for 618. She was finely appointed; the first-class restaurant was panelled in teak with a deck head that complemented the furniture, while the first-class bar was finished in grained pine with black leather furniture and brass and polished steel fittings.

Railways steamer *Falaise* (1946) seen here at anchor off St Malo. A number of summer cruises were carried out by the British in the post-war years.

Her first cruise duty took her to Amsterdam with a passenger complement of 320 on a weekend excursion from Harwich, which started on the 24 April 1964. She later visited Hamburg, Kiel and Copenhagen, and by 1966 she had been as far south as Lisbon, Oporto and Tangier. The arrival of newly built car ferries on the Harwich service in 1969 gave her greater opportunity for cruising, and between then and 1974, when the *Avalon* was herself converted for car carrying, she visited the Baltic, Sweden, France, Spain, Gibraltar and Morocco. She crossed the Arctic Circle and she even undertook a lengthy round-Britain autumn cruise.

Southern Ferries (part of what was then the General Steam Navigation Company, a P&O subsidiary) inaugurated the cruise ferry concept in the 1970s. They placed the *Eagle* on a new service between Southampton and Lisbon and also for a short trial onwards to Tangier. She had also been built with an eye to Caribbean cruising in the winter, but this never materialised. As a cruise ferry she had roll-on roll-off vehicle access at the stern, but also had large public rooms and a swimming pool. She was shortly joined by a partner, the *SF Panther*, an outdated ship that had been built for service in the Baltic in 1963. On the Lisbon ferry service and extended cruise to Tangier, the *Eagle* was ahead of her time and passage numbers could not be sustained. Indeed, she was never profitable and was sold in 1975. The competitive service offered by Swedish Lloyd, using the Swedish *Patricia* between Southampton and Bilbao, was also unsuccessful and withdrawn in the mid-1970s. By way of contrast the seasonal winter cruise ferry service operated to the Canaries by DFDS since 1966 (by the Danish registered *Black Watch* and *Black Prince*) was far more successful, allowing passengers to use the ship as a hotel while at the islands. The larger and British-registered *Blenheim* took over in 1970 until she was sold in 1981.

The concept was resurrected in the 1990s by P&O, who now maintain the *Pride of Bilbao* on a three-day return ferry crossing to Bilbao from Portsmouth. Brittany Ferries offered a similar service to Santander from Plymouth.

The *Eagle* (1972) is seen departing from Southampton for Lisbon in August 1973.

The *Blenheim* (1970) ran a successful winter-only cruise ferry service to the Canary Islands throughout the 1970s.

7

POST-WAR AUSTERITY

…sheets 31,000; pillow slips 31,000; table cloths 21,000; oven cloths 31,000; linen bags 2,200; bed slips, cabin class 3,500, third class 2,000; table cloths, cabin class 12,000, tourist class 6,000, third class 3,000; napkins, cabin class 74,000, tourist class 18,000; towels, cabin class 52,000, tourist class 20,000, third class 14,000; lavatory hand 80,000, roller 2,000, bath (white and red) 25,000, tourist (blue) 18,000; bath mats 2,400; afternoon tea cloths (coloured) 2,200; afternoon tea napkins (coloured) 9,000…

From the store's inventory of the *Queen Mary*.

In the late summer of 1939, liners, cruise ships, coastal liners and coastal cruise ships, ferries and even some of the butterfly boats were called up once again for active service. Many of these ships were lost during the hostilities of the Second World War (see Table 2) taking with them numerous seafarers and other personnel. The first passenger ship to be sunk was the Donaldson liner *Athenia*, torpedoed by a U-boat within hours of Britain and France declaring war on Germany on 3 September 1939. War raged for six long years and the ships and crews that survived entered a drab and austere post-war era in which men, materials and goods were scarce.

Happily, many of the great liners of the 1930s came through the war years relatively unscathed, but all were desperately in need of repair and rehabilitation. Whereas the Cunard Line's Queens had contributed greatly to the war effort as transports, the *Empress of Britain* was an early war loss. Other vessels such as the *Arandora Star* and two of her former sisters were lost; in the case of the *Arandora Star*, the contrast between her happy days as a cruise ship and the wartime circumstances of her loss could not have been greater. She was torpedoed 120km west of Ireland with the loss of 761 lives. In a letter to *Sea Breezes*, dated February 1971, D. Robertson of Holyhead records:

I joined the ship as an Able Seaman in Liverpool shortly before her trip to Narvik and served throughout her rescue and evacuation operations until she was finally torpedoed and sunk off the Irish coast on 3 July 1940. After the torpedo struck the ship I lowered the starboard launch and assisted in lowering one lifeboat. The appalling conditions did engender a degree of panic. I can vividly recall a number of Italian internees clinging desperately to empty boat falls as the ship heeled over. The screams of fear can be imagined. I found my salvation by launching a raft, jumping overboard and

Seen at Southampton in 1946 the *Queen Mary* (1936) still sports her drab wartime colours whilst the *Queen Elizabeth* (1940) has already received her civilian paintwork.

The Donaldson Line's *Athenia* (1923) was torpedoed hours into the Second World War with the loss of 112 lives. Nearly 1,300 survivors were picked up.

swimming to it. I managed to help on board seven other survivors who were adrift in the water, before we were rescued nine hours later by the Canadian destroyer *St Laurent*.

Many of the newer ships dating from the late 1930s did survive and the liner companies were able to resume commercial services once vessels were released from duty. These included Cunard's *Mauretania*, Royal Mail's *Andes*, a number of the Union-Castle liners including the *Stirling Castle*, *Athlone Castle* and *Capetown Castle*, all but two of the P&O and Orient Line's Strath- and Orcades-class, and Shaw Savill Line's *Dominion Monarch*. Three of the four Dunera-class troopships, including Bibby Line's *Devonshire*, also survived, P&O's *Ettrick* being torpedoed by a U-boat in November 1942.

The *Mauretania* was notable, although always overshadowed by her great partners, the *Queen Mary* and *Queen Elizabeth*. Designed with an eye to off-season cruising, the new *Mauretania* was an impressive-looking vessel with two large funnels placed slightly forward of centre, giving her an unbalanced profile. She was delivered in time to start work in June 1939 and completed only four return transatlantic trips before being stripped of her finery to become a troopship. On her inaugural arrival in New York with 1,300 passengers and under the command of Captain A.T. Brown (who had delivered her namesake to the breakers' yard in Rosyth in 1935), the *New York Times* reported:

> That she should be built at all in this critical period of world affairs testifies to the courage of her owners and their faith in the future of our two great democracies.

The new *Mauretania* had a high speed of 23 knots, so that she could deputise for the Queens (an eventuality that never actually materialised), and was designed to supplement the London to New York service alongside the *Britannic* and *Georgic* with a winter role as a cruise ship. These duties had been taken from her almost as soon as she arrived on station.

A number of ships were not worth repairing after the war whilst others were converted to become emigrant ships providing Government-assisted passages to Australia and New Zealand. The *Monarch of Bermuda* became the *New Australia* for the Ministry of Transport, whilst a number of other vessels that had been involved with cruising in the 1930s also became post-war emigrant ships. These were the Orient Line's *Ormonde*, Henderson Line's *Amarapoora*, the Cunard-White Star Lines' *Georgic*, Royal Mail's *Asturias* and their former cruise ship *Atlantis* (formerly *Andes*).

Shortage of tonnage and a total absence of licenses to build passenger ships during the war years meant that companies needed to build new ships as quickly as constraints on materials, labour and money would allow. Building costs had risen considerably over pre-war prices, but a flurry of new ships emerged from the builders' yards between 1947 and 1950. For the most part the ships were based on pre-war designs so that most could be described as unimaginative, even bland. These included P&O's *Himalaya* and *Chusan* and the Orient Line's new *Orcades*, which were developments of the 1930s Strath-class of liner, the New Zealand Line's *Rangitoto* and *Rangitane*, the Union-Castle Line's *Pretoria Castle* and *Edinburgh Castle* and the Royal Mail liner *Magdalena*. The latter vessel was laid down in 1946 and completed only in 1948 as materials were still scarce, but was wrecked the following year in good visibility off Rio de Janeiro. This was a serious blow to the proud Merchant Navy and one for which the master was described at the subsequent inquiry to be in 'grave dereliction of duty'. The aftermath of the tragedy was described by D. King-Page in a letter to the editor of *Sea Breezes* in July 1949:

Former two-funnelled liner and cruise ship, pictured here as emigrant ship *Asturias* (1926) setting off for the Antipodes. The card was posted in 1950 and with the message: 'Dear Mother and Father, I am sending this from Malta where we are calling but not allowed to land. There are five other girls in with me in my cabin… Will write from Australia…'

> She [the *Magdalena*] was refloated and was being towed into port when she took a sheer while passing over the bar in a heavy swell, and fell into the trough of the seas, pounding on the bottom so heavily that she broke in two. The forepart sank, and the afterpart was beached nearby, and for a time there was talk of refloating it, making it seaworthy, and towing it to a British repair yard, but this has proved impracticable.

Few owners were then contemplating building cruise ships. However, two notable vessels were completed, both aimed primarily at the American cruise market. These were the *Caronia*, built by John Brown on Clydeside for the Cunard Line, and the *Ocean Monarch* (see Chapter 5), built by Vickers Armstrong at Barrow and delivered to the Furness Bermuda Line in 1951 as a replacement for the *Monarch of Bermuda*.

The cruise liner *Caronia* was built as a summer transatlantic partner for the *Mauretania* and a luxury winter cruise ship. This vessel possessed all the innovation that was lacking elsewhere. That the board of the Cunard-White Star Line had the vision of such grandeur and magnificence at all in the post-war gloom is all the more remarkable. Cunard went back to John Brown's yard on the Clyde for this ship, where she was launched by Princess Elizabeth on 30 October 1947, carrying a special livery comprising shades of pale green.

Although she was even stumpier than the *Empress of Britain* or the *Queen of Bermuda* (in order to facilitate access to confined harbours), the 'Green Goddess' *Caronia* possessed a beauty of her own. Her massive central superstructure was crowned by a single oversize funnel and a single mast behind the bridge. She was a two-class ship with no tourist accommodation, and she carried 581 first-class and 351 cabin-class passengers on liner voyages or 600 one-class passengers on cruises.

The *Caronia* (1948) as built, and returning to Southampton from a cruise in 1965.

Her crew of 600 provided a one-to-one ratio of crew to cruise passengers. With a gross tonnage of 34,172, she was the largest liner to be purpose-built with a dual cruising liner role and the largest single funnel ship yet built. Contemporary descriptions include the following:

> The passenger accommodation is of particularly high standard, both as regards its appointments and in its decorative art. The first-class public rooms comprise observation lounge, cocktail bar lounge, writing room, smoking room, library, garden lounges, restaurant and a cinema with seating for 300. There is also a gymnasium and a veranda café on the Sports Deck, overlooking the open-air lido and swimming pool on the Sun Deck.

The *Caronia* took her maiden voyage in January 1947. Every cabin had its own bathroom (not the case even in first class on the *Queen Mary* and *Queen Elizabeth*), the sun decks were vast and uncluttered and there was a permanent outside swimming pool. Her public rooms reflected the art deco style and were finished to a standard as yet unequalled on any liner, with much use made of traditional polished wood finishes, rich colours and high-quality furnishings. She was not, however, targeted at cash-starved Britain, but set sail on a dull January day for New York to start taking dollars from the richer Americans in return for her services.

The *Mauretania* had been returned to her builders, Cammell Laird, in September 1946 for refurbishment and was ready for her first post-war transatlantic voyage on 26 April 1947. Her original fittings had to be gathered from stores not only in Liverpool but also from New York and Sydney, so hurriedly had she been pressed into war service. J.H. Isherwood reported in *Sea Breezes* in November 1986:

When the refit was completed Cunard invited civic and industrial representatives, and members of the firms engaged in the work, for a short 2½ day cruise in their renovated liner. She left Liverpool on 18 April 1947 but when to the north of Skye the weather became so threatening that she turned back towards the Mersey.

On 21 April she was off the Mersey Bar but the gale was then too bad for her to enter the river and she was taken off to an allegedly safe anchorage in Moelfre Bay. Here, however, she dragged her anchors and had to be taken out to sea to ride out the gale. It was 24 April before she got back into the Mersey and her sailing date was 26 April! Nevertheless, after a tremendous rush she managed to get away to New York on schedule.

She was to become the partner to the *Caronia*, and the *Mauretania* commenced her own winter cruise programme out of New York in 1947. That first winter she made five cruises from New York to Nassau, La Guaira, Curaçao, Colon and Havana.

The *Britannic* was released back to Cunard in March 1947, although she was no longer destined to partner the *Mauretania* as had been the plan in 1939. The *Britannic* was sent to Harland & Wolff at Liverpool to be refitted as a two-class ship for the Liverpool to New York service, duties which she finally took up in May 1948. The passenger and crew accommodation was entirely reconstructed and decoration throughout was in keeping with her new role as a winter cruise ship. New shops were added, a new swimming pool was built on C-deck and most cabins were provided with toilets. Cruising highlights for the *Britannic* included a fifty-nine-day, twenty-two-port cruise of the Mediterranean in January 1953, which was repeated two years later. Finally, her old and outdated air-injection diesel machinery caught up with her, and coupled with crankshaft damage at New York, the old ship sailed to the breakers' yard in 1960. However, to the very last, the *Britannic* proudly wore the colours of the White Star Line rather than the red and black of Cunard, and with her passing went the last ship to fly the White Star Line house flag.

The *Britannic* (1930) proudly wore the colours of the White Star Line to the last.

First-class cocktail lounge aboard the *Britannic.*

The *Britannic*'s tourist-class dining saloon.

Canadian Pacific survived the war with only the *Duchess of Bedford* and *Duchess of Richmond*, other than its fleet of cargo ships. In 1947 the two Duchesses were elevated to Empress status and became the *Empress of France* and *Empress of Canada* respectively. They were joined by the former *Empress of Japan*, commissioned in 1930 for the transpacific route and renamed *Empress of Scotland* during the war when Japan took sides. Giving up the Pacific service it was left to these three ships to inaugurate the post-war transatlantic service. The *Empress of Scotland* was completely

The *Empress of Scotland* (1930) inaugurated Canadian Pacific's post-war cruise programme.

refurbished between 1948 and 1950, and when she finally left the Clyde she was all but a new ship. After her first few transatlantic trips a 17-ton swimming pool module was hoisted aboard and she set sail in December 1950 for New York and the Caribbean, providing the company's first post-war cruises.

In 1951 the *Empress of Scotland* made six New York cruises and one from Southampton. Before she was displaced by the new liners *Empress of England* and *Empress of Britain* in 1957, the *Empress of Scotland* made twenty-six cruises from New York to the Caribbean, normally of fourteen- to sixteen-days duration, two from Southampton and one from Southampton to South America. By way of example, she left Liverpool for Southampton and Cherbourg in December 1953 for a month in the South Atlantic, with fares ranging from £240 to £795. Returning to Southampton on 18 January she was then rostered to carry out three Caribbean cruises from New York before returning to liner duties. The old *Empress of Scotland* was sold in 1957 for further service as the *Hanseatic* for the Hamburg Atlantic Line, her cruise ship role initially taken by the new *Empress of Britain*. From 1961 onwards the winter cruise ship became the *Empress of Canada*, the very last of the Canadian Pacific liners but, like her predecessor the *Empress of Britain* of 1930, built as a dual cruise liner (see Chapter 8). However, from 1962 onwards all three new Empresses were employed on winter cruising.

By the late 1950s the Cunarder *Caronia* had become a dedicated cruise ship with only an occasional positioning run across the Atlantic. She arrived in New York from annual refit in the UK in early January, ready for her annual three-month round-the-world cruise. There was then a spring-time Mediterranean cruise followed by a summer cruise to Scandinavia and the North Cape, followed by another cruise to the Mediterranean. This allowed time to return from New York to the UK for her late autumn dry-docking and refit before resuming again the following January. Passengers arrived at the pier in New York with countless pieces of baggage, including several wardrobe trunks, and the ship even offered a cold storage room for the ladies' fur coats. Bill Miller wrote in his book *British Ocean Liners*:

1 The *Orsova* (1909) was used for off-season cruising in the 1920s, seen here proudly flying the Blue Ensign, from a classic painting by Charles Dixon.

2 The classic art card of the cruise liner *Carinthia* (1925), from a painting by Kenneth Shoesmith.

3 The grandly titled Royal Mail Steam Yacht *Atlantis* (1913), from an art card painted by John Fay.

4   The Booth Line's *Hilary*
(1931) seen on the Amazon,
from a company art card.

5   The White Star Line's
Majestic (1922), from a
painting by Charles Dixon,
which carried out a number
of New York to Bermuda
cruises.

6 The *Monarch of Bermuda* (1931), from an art card painted by C. Hopkins.

7 The *Aquitania* (1914), from a painting by Frank Mason.

8 The *Letitia* (1925) was built for the Donaldson Line Transatlantic service with an eye to winter cruising to the Mediterranean.

9   The Blue Funnel Line's *Nestor* (1913) seen here, and *Ulysses* (1913) offered all-inclusive tours to the Great Barrier Reef throughout the 1930s as part of their liner duties between the UK and Australia.

10   The second *Coronia* (1935) to be based at Scarborough. She brought 900 soldiers back from the Dunkirk beaches in June 1940 and is one of the few Dunkirk survivors still in operation.

11 The *Pride of Bilbao* (1986) seen off Southsea during the August Bank Holiday weekend, 2006.

12 The *Waverley* (1947) carries on the tradition of seasonal day excursions by paddle steamer – 'weather and other circumstances permitting'.

13 The 'Love Boat' – Princess Cruises' *Pacific Princess* (1971). (Carnival Corporation)

14 The end of the liner service – the *Edinburgh Castle* (1948) seen arriving at Cape Town from Southampton in January 1970.

15 The first of a new generation of cruise ships was the *Royal Princess* (1984), seen during a cruise to 'New England'. (Carnival Corporation)

16 Horizon Lounge, *Royal Princess*. (Carnival Corporation)

17 The very last British steam turbine-driven passenger ship, the *Sky Princess* (1984), now operating from Australia as the *Pacific Sky*. (Carnival Corporation)

18 Horizon Lounge, *Pacific Sky*. (Carnival Corporation)

19　The *Sun Princess* (1995) on an Alaskan cruise. (Carnival Corporation)

20　The casino aboard the *Sun Princess*. (Carnival Corporation)

21 Opposite above: The *Dawn Princess* (1997) seen on an Alaskan cruise. (Carnival Corporation)

22 Opposite below: The *Caronia* (1973) at the Dover Cruise Terminal.

23 Right: The *Sea Princess* (1998) at sea. (Carnival Corporation)

24 Below: The *Aurora* (2000) off Calshot Spit on 10 June 2006.

25   The Horizon Court aboard the *Sea Princess*. (Carnival Corporation)

26   The *Artemis* (1984) passing Calshot Spit on 29 April 2006 with Hamilton, Bermuda, as her port of registry.

27 The British-registered *Saga Ruby* (1973) seen passing Calshot Spit on 10 June 2006.

28 The *Lord of the Glens* (1985) in the Caledonian Canal at the head of Neptune's Staircase, Banavie, awaiting her passengers' return from a shore excursion.

29 P&O Cruises *Adonia* (1998) seen in Southampton Water at the start of a summer cruise in May 2004.

30 Sadly flagged-out to the Bermudan registry, the new *Arcadia* (2005) makes an impressive sight off Calshot Castle in April 2006.

31   The International Show Lounge aboard the *Crown Princess*. (Carnival Corporation)

32   The *Queen Mary 2* (2003) off Calshot Castle, Southampton Water, in July 2007.

33 The *Ocean Village Two* (1997) passes Calshot Spit in April 2007, inbound to Southampton from Bremerhaven following conversion from *AIDAblu*, formerly *Dawn Princess*.

34 The *Queen Elizabeth 2* (1969) in Norway, August 2007. (Richard Danielson)

The *Camito* (1956) departing from Southampton for the West Indies in June 1968.

The *Caronia* had a devoted, club-like following of passengers, some of whom lived aboard for several years at a time. The ports of call became less important (some passengers, in fact, rarely went ashore) as the ship was a superbly run, completely comfortable and totally secure 'floating resort'. Cunard's finest and usually most senior staff served aboard the *Caronia*.

The *Mauretania* continued in her role as summer liner and winter cruise ship, receiving full air conditioning in 1958. However, by 1962 she was a full-time cruise ship like the *Caronia*, and in recognition her hull was adorned in the same shades of pastel green, Cunard's cruising green. The *Mauretania's* big sisters, the *Queen Mary* and *Queen Elizabeth*, were also of necessity turning to winter cruising, such was the competition from air travel; the *Queen Mary* took her first cruise in 1963 (see Chapter 8).

During the 1950s, opportunity to enjoy dedicated cruises based on UK ports were few, but the off-season cruises by Cunard and Canadian Pacific to the Mediterranean and occasionally the Caribbean were generally well patronised. The traditional liner voyages to the Caribbean by Elders & Fyffes on the banana run continued to develop a following. In 1949 the new steamer, *Golfito*, joined the fleet, complete with large lounges, ballroom, swimming pool, smoking room bar, shop, hairdressers and library, and with berths for 111 first-class passengers. She was joined in 1956 by near sister, the *Camito*, when the last of the old-style, pre-war passenger vessels the *Ariguani*, *Bayano* and *Cavina* were withdrawn. The passenger service was closed in 1973, but it was still possible to travel on a banana boat as one of only ten or twelve passengers aboard ships of the Geest Line, which operated out of Barry. The accommodation on the Geest ships had the passenger saloon, bar and lounge laid out across the full width of the fore end of the bridge deck.

The *Iberia* (1954) in cruising mode at Southampton in June 1967.

Longer voyages were available on the African and Australian services, but P&O and the Orient Line both concentrated their post-war efforts on the emigrant trade, although first-class round-trippers were always welcome. Orient Line cruises resumed in 1951 using the *Orion*, and latterly the newly completed *Orcades*, when a two-week cruise to Norway cost between £40 and £65, a threefold increase over 1930s prices.

Companies such as the Booth Line continued to woo passengers up the Amazon, whilst the Royal Mail Group would show you the exotic delights of the South America west coast run. The 1950s, however, demonstrated a reluctance of cruise passengers to be at sea for more than a week or so, and the popularity of these longer cruise opportunities waned. Besides, the average disposable income needed to buy them was no longer available, and lengthy holidays became a thing of the past. However, by the early 1960s the economic recovery of the UK again allowed access to some of the more interesting liner voyages, and the popularity of cruising on a liner to West Africa or through the Panama Canal increased once more.

One company that was aware of the round-trip market was Elder Dempster, with their Liverpool to West Africa sailings providing a round trip of four and a half weeks. Elder Dempster had lost all their newer passenger ships in the war and rapidly ordered two new builds from Vickers Armstrong, the *Accra* and *Apapa*, based on the pre-war design of the *Abosso* which had been delivered in 1935 but was lost in the war. The new ships were delivered in 1947 and 1948 and enabled the West African passenger service to resume with departures every three weeks. A third ship was ordered in March 1949, this time from Alexander Stephen on the Clyde. Time was now available to design a modern ship fit for a new era, and from the young company chairman, John Joyce, and his naval architect John Waddington, came the elegant but practical *Aureol*.

The *Aureol* was some 30 metres longer than her two running mates and her profile was yacht-like and beautifully set-off by an all white hull and a simple yellow funnel. She cost £1.8 million to build, and could accommodate 269 first-class and 100 cabin-class passengers. First-class

Yacht Holidays of London River Rhine cruiser *Lady Elizabeth* (1955) at Rotterdam.

The *Aureol* (1951) seen in the Mersey in 1966 preparing for another liner voyage to West Africa.

cabins were all fitted with integral bathrooms, and there were four large suites available. Facilities including a swimming pool, shops and two hairdressers, plus all the features expected of a modern passenger liner, including a children's area. Following a shakedown cruise off Scotland, she was loaded ready for her maiden voyage on 8 November 1951.

Unlike the *Accra* and *Apapa*, the *Aureol* was part air-conditioned – this was upgraded in 1960. So it was that the *Aureol* began to be marketed as a holiday ship, and in this role she developed a considerable trade in round-trip cruise passengers and cruises to Las Palmas with passengers returning by *Accra* or *Apapa* to Liverpool. The service was second to none, with extensive menus, ice cream available on deck throughout the day, and organised entertainment such as bridge schools and bingo as well as the normal deck games.

Although the older pair was withdrawn in the late 1960s, the *Aureol*, affectionately referred to on Merseyside as 'The White Swan', continued until 1974 when the service was withdrawn. The *Aureol* undertook some dedicated cruises in 1967, but these were not a success – clearly the attraction of the West African working voyage was greater than that of the ship herself. At the time of her withdrawal from the West African service, the poor-quality steel available to ship builders in the post-war years was beginning to show signs of deterioration and maintenance costs were increasing. However, the ship lasted until 2001, serving as an accommodation vessel and later was laid up for many years at Piraeus.

The Union-Castle Line also marketed round-trip voyages, principally on their East African run through the Mediterranean and the Suez Canal but also on the round-Africa service. The round-Africa service was maintained by the *Warwick Castle* and the *Durban Castle* until the route

Always popular on the East African run as a cruise venue was the Union-Castle Line's *Rhodesia Castle* (1951). (FotoFlite)

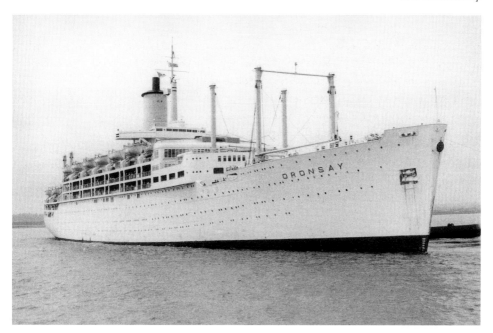

The *Oronsay* (1951) berthing at the Western Docks in Southampton in 1969.

was withdrawn in 1960. However, advertising latterly brought only a modest response from round-trip passengers.

The East African service was run in competition with British India Line. British India had the two-class liners, the *Uganda* and *Kenya*, placed new on the service out of London in 1951 and 1952 respectively. These were better appointed but more formal passenger vessels than their one-class Union-Castle Line counterparts (the *Rhodesia Castle*, *Kenya Castle* and *Braemar Castle*), which had also been completed in 1951 and 1952. The two services remained popular with tourist passengers, particularly in the 1960s, until the closure of the Suez Canal in 1967 spelled the end. The last voyage was that of the *Kenya* in the early summer of 1969. The *Uganda* went on to become the last of the school ships, surviving in this role until 1982 (see Chapter 8).

Other cruising initiatives in the 1950s were closer to home, and were undertaken by Coast Lines and latterly British Railways with the *Lady Killarney* and the *Duke of Lancaster* respectively (see Chapter 6). Day cruises by Eagle Steamers on the Thames, P&A Campbell on the Bristol Channel, the paddle steamers and turbine steamers of the Clyde and the steamers of the Liverpool and North Wales Steam Packet Company were attracting (fair-weather) capacity patronage. However, their popularity was soon to decline almost to a point of extinction.

Seasonal river cruising up the Rhine as far as Switzerland was then possible under the Red Ensign with Yacht Holidays Ltd of Buckingham Palace Road, London. Three ships had been used before the war in competition with the established Dutch and German fleets. There were four ships in service in the 1950s and these were extremely popular with British tourists. The trip upriver to Basle was scheduled to take sixty-three hours and the return trip only thirty-four hours. The service thrived on a British crew providing British tourists with top-quality food and attention.

THE CUNARD LINE

Although Samuel Cunard is generally credited with the foundation of the Cunard Line in 1839, his acknowledgement might not have been so widely given but for the distinctiveness of his name. The idea of a fortnightly steam sailing to and from North America was certainly that of Cunard. However, co-signatories of the contract with the British Government that established the original British and North American Royal Mail Steam Packet Company were the Scottish shipowners David McIver and George Burns. McIver and Burns were also responsible for much of the initial capital outlay that created the company. A third Scot was instrumental in the success of the company by recognising the physical difficulties of maintaining a twice-monthly service and in specifying ships that were capable of the job, both in size and power and in number. This was the famous Clyde engineer Robert Napier, designer of the four Clyde-built Britannia-class paddle steamers, each of 1,154 tons gross.

The British & North American Company thrived until competition was such that the Government subsidy was at first halved, and then in the 1870s taken away altogether. It was at this point, when major reconstruction of the company was taking place, driven by the sale of shares, that a new company name was considered. Something distinctive and proud was needed, but neither the Burns nor the McIver Steamship Company had quite the ring that the Cunard Steamship Company offered. Sadly thereafter, the Scottish foundation of the company was lost to the marginal Anglo-Nova Scotian roots of Samuel Cunard (the family name 'Cunard' being an anglicised derivative of the German name 'Kunard', and not as some Gaelic speakers would have it reflecting the words 'cuan ard' – the high seas).

From the outset the policy of the Cunard Line was one of caution – speed-with-comfort and safety – leaving other companies to experiment with unproven technology. Even the 1930s Queens were more orthodox and less luxurious than many of the other great liners of the day, the French Line's *Normandie*, for example. The only exceptions to this policy were the greyhounds *Lusitania* and *Mauretania*, both completed in 1907. At that time the American financier J.P. Morgan was buying up the North Atlantic shipping lines to form his International Mercantile Marine Company. Bruce Ismay was forced by his shareholders to sell the White Star Line. Lord Inverclyde, George Arbuthnot Burns and grandson of George Burns, now in charge of Cunard, had gone to the Government and canvassed a £2.6 million loan in return for building the biggest, most luxurious and fastest ships on the high seas. Armed with the protection of the loan, Morgan had been unable to get his clutches on the Cunard Line, and in true win-win style the Cunard Line found itself the operators of a pair of crack four-funnellers.

In 1927 the Royal Mail Group determined to restore the White Star Line to British ownership, but paid dearly for it. With the subsequent failure of the Royal Mail Group and its enigmatic leader, Lord Kylsant, the Cunard Line was only able to secure a further Government loan, this time for £3 million, in order to complete the *Queen Mary*, conditional on its amalgamation with the White Star Line. The holding company, Cunard White Star, was formed on 1 January 1934, but in 1947 the Cunard Line eliminated the name White Star Line by purchasing the holding company and reverting to the name of Cunard Steamship Company.

Today the Cunard Line is wholly American owned, surviving as a cruise ship brand within the mighty Carnival Corporation. Its Scottish ancestry is now long forgotten.

TABLE 2: PASSENGER VESSELS (EXCLUDING DAY-EXCURSION SHIPS), PREVIOUSLY USED AS FULL OR PART-TIME CRUISE SHIPS, LOST IN THE SECOND WORLD WAR

A: (1) Requisitioned as Armed Merchant Cruisers, (2) Ocean Boarding Vessel, (3) Store carrier, (4) Fleet Air Arm Target Vessel, (5) Convoy Rescue Ship

Name	Former owners	Date of loss	How lost
Carinthia (1)	Cunard-White Star	7 June 1940	U-boat torpedo, west of Ireland
Vandyck (2)	Lamport & Holt	10 June 1940	Air attack near Narvik
Transylvania (1)	Anchor Line	10 August 1940	U-boat torpedo, north of Ireland
Laurentic (1)	Cunard-White Star	3 November 1940	U-boat torpedo, NW Approaches
Voltaire (1)	Lamport & Holt	4 April 1941	Surface raider, mid-Atlantic
Ulster Prince (3)	Belfast Steamship	25 April 1941	Bombed lying aground during evacuation from Greece
Camito (2)	Elders & Fyffes	6 May 1941	U-boat torpedo, N Atlantic
St Briac (4)	Southern Railway	12 March 1942	Mined off Aberdeen
St Sunniva (5)	North of Scotland Co.	22 January 1943	As Convoy Rescue Ship, lost due to severe icing

B: Merchant Vessels

Name	Company	Date of Loss	How Lost
Carare	Elders & Fyffes	28 May 1940	Mined, Bristol Channel
Orford	Orient Line	1 June 1940	Bombed by aircraft, Marseilles
Lancastria	Cunard-White Star	17 June 1940	Bombed by aircraft, St Nazaire
Arandora Star	Blue Star Line	2 July 1940	U-boat torpedo, west of Ireland
Kemmendine	Henderson Line	13 July 1940	Surface raider, Indian Ocean
Empress of Britain	Canadian Pacific	28 October 1940	Aircraft and U-boat torpedo attack, NW of Ireland
Inanda	Harrison Line	7 September 1940	Bombed by aircraft, London
Incosi	Harrison Line	7 September 1940	Bombed by aircraft, London
Innisfallen	City of Cork	21 December 1940	Mined in River Mersey
City of Nagpur	Ellerman	29 April 1941	U-boat torpedo, west of Fastnet
Nerissa	Bermuda & West Indies SS	30 April 1941	U-boat torpedo, north-west of Ireland
Anselm	Booth Line	5 July 1941	U-boat torpedo
Aguila	Yeoward Bros.	19 August 1941	U-boat torpedo, off Portugal
Avoceta	Yeoward Bros.	21 September 1941	U-boat torpedo, off France
Ulysses	Blue Funnel Line	11 April 1942	U-boat torpedo, off Florida
Laconia	Cunard-White Star	12 September 1942	U-boat torpedo, off Liberia
Oronsay	Orient Line	9 October 1942	U-boat torpedo, south-west of Monrovia
Duchess of Atholl	Canadian Pacific	10 October 1942	U-boat torpedo, east of Ascension Island
Orcades	Orient Line	10 October 1942	U-boat torpedo, South Atlantic
Ardeola	Yeoward Bros.	9 November 1942	Captured off Bizerta
Viceroy of India	P&O	11 November 1942	U-boat torpedo, off Oran
Strathallan	P&O	21 December 1942	U-boat torpedo, off Algeria
California	Anchor Line	11 July 1943	Bombed by aircraft, west of Portugal
Duchess of York	Canadian Pacific	11 July 1943	Bombed by aircraft, west of Portugal
Neuralia	British India	1 May 1945	Mined (Allied mine) in Gulf of Taranto

8

PART-TIME CRUISE SHIPS AND REDUNDANT LINERS

The future of the large transatlantic liner is difficult to predict. It seems that ships of the *Queen Elizabeth*'s size and capacity will gradually diminish. The increase of air traffic is making it difficult to maintain such great ships on an economic basis. Ships of lesser tonnages are not faced with this same problem, however, and there is no danger of passenger liners becoming completely extinct.

From *Ships*, edited by Robina Farbrother, Paul Hamlyn Ltd, London, 1963.

Following the mad scramble for new passenger and cargo tonnage in the immediate post-war years, a determined and steady demand for new liners continued throughout the 1950s. Materials had become more freely available, but shipbuilding costs were rising. Fuel oil was still modestly priced and so the steam turbine remained the preferred means of power, although considerably modified with the development of the Pametrada-type turbines which incorporated many of the American wartime military improvements.

A number of companies built new liners in the 1950s that were later to take a dominant role in the burgeoning cruise market in the UK. They included Canadian Pacific, Cunard, Pacific Steam Navigation Company, P&O, Orient Line, Shaw Savill and British India. Of these, the Canadian Pacific, Cunard and the Orient Line were actively engaged in offering cruises throughout the 1950s, the other companies joining them of necessity, as demand for long sea passages ebbed at the hands of the aeroplane from the early 1960s onwards.

In addition there were some notable vessels built for other companies, including Union-Castle's *Pendennis Castle*, the Ellerman & Bucknall Line's four sisters of the City of Port Elizabeth-class, and the three Royal Mail Line Graces of the Amazon-class which displaced the pre-war-built *Andes*. None of these were involved in cruising, largely because of their massive refrigerated cargo spaces and the prohibitive costs of conversion to passenger-only service. Nevertheless, the Ellerman & Bucknall 'Cities' offered very attractive 'short holiday voyages' during the 1960s, from Middlesbrough to Rotterdam, Hamburg and sometimes Antwerp, whilst the ships followed their normal cargo-handling circuit preparatory to leaving London for South Africa.

Of the North Atlantic liners that came out in the 1950s, the four Cunarders were noteworthy; *Saxonia* and *Ivernia* were built principally for the Southampton (and London also in winter)-based Canadian service, and the *Carinthia* and *Sylvania* were constructed for the Liverpool and

The *Carinthia* (1956) at Liverpool in 1966.

The *Carinthia*'s tourist-class children's playroom – contrast this with the picture of the first-class children's playroom aboard the *Empress of Britain* (1931) on page 39.

Greenock service to Canada. They were all of the same design, with the first pair ordered in 1951, and came from John Brown at Clydebank between 1954 and 1957. The design with fully enclosed decks was dictated by the rigours of 'Winter North Atlantic'. They were very successful, using Quebec and Montreal as their Canadian terminals in summer and Halifax and New York in winter. They even had a distinctive recessed 5-ton stern anchor for use in the confined approaches to Quebec. However, passenger numbers soon waned in the winter months with competition from the airlines, and it was not long before a winter cruise ship role was adopted.

The Cinema Theatre aboard the *Carinthia*.

The post-war experience of the Cunard Line illustrates how liner tonnage slowly took on the dual role of cruising. The early commercial career of the *Mauretania* included a cruising schedule during the winter months (see Chapter 7). In 1962 she was painted in the distinctive cruising green livery, and in 1964 she took up a cruising programme from Southampton although her final voyage was again from New York, terminating at Southampton in November 1965. Her main cruising partner from New York was the Green Goddess, the *Caronia*. However, throughout her career the *Mauretania* was dogged with mechanical problems, particularly her turbine gearing.

There was an incident during the Cuban missile crisis in 1962 when the *Caronia* was scheduled to make her very first call at Yalta in the Black Sea. She left New York on 5 October, fully loaded with a largely American passenger list (the fares started at £393 for the cruise which returned to New York at the end of November). On entering Russian waters she suddenly found herself surrounded by six Soviet gunboats. President Kennedy had just told the Russian President, Mr Krushchev, to withdraw his ships from Cuba; the situation was tense. The *Caronia* was allowed to dock while many of the American passengers made themselves scarce aboard ship. The next day the *Caronia* was escorted out to sea to resume her cruise, much to the relief of many on board.

The *Caronia*-style green livery was given to the intermediate liners *Saxonia*, when she was renamed the *Carmania*, and *Ivernia*, which became the *Franconia* following a major refit in 1963. The refits cost £2 million and included the provision of a lido deck and swimming pool at the expense of the after-holds, hatches and cargo handling gear, plus the installation of air conditioning throughout. They were also given distillation plants to produce fresh water at sea, and larger fuel bunkers to increase their cruising range. Although retained on the Canadian service in summer, they were then put on a winter cruise schedule which was focused on the lucrative Caribbean market. In the first winter after their refit the *Carmania* made seven Caribbean cruises out of Port Everglades, whilst the *Franconia* made the same number of cruises to the Caribbean from New York.

The *Carmania* (1954) returning from a cruise to berth at the Ocean Terminal at Southampton in May 1969.

The *Sylvania* and *Carinthia* were also upgraded for off-season cruising in the winter of 1963–64, although not with the same thoroughness as the *Carmania* and *Franconia*. Even the *Queen Elizabeth* was dealt with in this manner two winters later. It was also announced that the proposed replacement for the *Queen Mary* (the *Queen Elizabeth 2*) would be designed, like the *Caronia* before her, as a dual-purpose liner and cruise ship. The first Cunard cruise from the Mersey since 1939 began on 10 February 1965 when the *Sylvania* set off on a twenty-seven-day cruise to the Mediterranean. UK departures were otherwise based at Southampton.

The *Sylvania*, which had adopted an all-white livery for cruising, and the *Carinthia*, along with the *Caronia*, were withdrawn and sold in 1968. The *Caronia* undertook only a few cruises for her new owners and was sold for demolition in 1974, but sank at Guam whilst being towed to the breakers' yard in Taiwan. The *Queen Elizabeth* completed her final voyage for Cunard, also in 1968, and she too met with a violent end, ablaze in Hong Kong harbour as the *Seawise University*. The *Franconia* and *Carmania* were dedicated to cruising from 1967 onwards, the *Franconia* picking up for a short while the New York to Bermuda service, now abandoned by the Furness Bermuda Line (see Chapter 4). Eventually laid up in 1971 following a manning dispute with the National Union of Seamen, the two ships were put up for sale.

Of the many stories relating to these ships, that of the repair of the leaking starboard propeller gland on the *Franconia* during a Mediterranean cruise on Christmas Eve 1967 is, perhaps, one of the more memorable. With 700 passengers expecting their cruise to continue on from Tangier over the holiday period and no dockyard facilities available, Captain Phil Read and a senior engineer donned diving gear and went down to seal the outside of the propeller shaft in polythene. This allowed the ship's engineers to replace the leaking gland. Whether the captain was applauded by his passengers for actions over and above the call of duty is not recorded, but a note of gratitude was sent to him by the owners.

Canadian Pacific brought out the slightly faster (20½ knots) and slightly larger vessels the *Empress of Britain* and *Empress of England* in 1956 and 1957. The *Empress of Britain* adopted the

The first cruise from Southampton by the *Empress of Canada* (1961) started on 21 October 1969. She is seen wearing the green and white CP Ships livery rather than the traditional yellow funnel and chequer board colours.

winter cruise ship role whilst her sister maintained a one-ship transatlantic service. The *Empress of Britain* was displaced from cruising when a third ship, the *Empress of Canada*, joined the fleet in 1961. Similar to the earlier ships and with identical turbine engines, she was 3 metres longer than they were and ½ metre broader in the beam, and this gave her a slower service speed of 20 knots. The new ship was designed as a liner and cruise ship and had more first-class berths (192) and a range of second-class cabins that doubled as one-class cruise accommodation.

A significant boost to cruising from UK ports aboard British-registered ships was the currency restrictions in force throughout most of the 1960s and into the 1970s, which limited tourists to exporting only £50 per year. Money spent on fares and aboard a British ship was money spent at home, so the £50 was entirely available for shore-side excursions during the cruise.

Although none of the Cunarders and Canadian Pacific liners were built for sunshine cruising, all of them spent the majority of their careers in this role, either under the Red or Blue Ensigns or later under foreign flags. Better equipped for sunshine cruising were the liners built for the P&O and Orient Line fleets in the 1950s, and most of these spent their later years as cruise ships within the combined P&O-Orient management, which became P&O Cruises in 1973. P&O built the near sisters *Arcadia* and *Iberia* for the India and Australian service, and Orient Line constructed the *Oronsay* and *Orsova* for the direct London to Australia and transpacific routes. They were fast ships, each capable of maintaining 22 knots on their long trek to Australia, and they were designed for hot weather work. They were built with nearly as many first-class berths as tourist-class, and even though they had significant cargo capacity they were ideal vessels for a secondary cruising role or for permanent conversion to cruise ships.

The career of the *Orsova* (1954) as a cruise ship ended in 1973 when P&O decided to dispose of it in favour of the *Canberra*.

Some of the earlier post-war builds were disposed of as unsuitable for conversion, although ships such as the *Orcades* did carry out a few cruises. The *Orsova* carried out a number of cruises in her final years, and the *Oronsay* had a highly successful West Coast of America cruise season in 1972, mainly to Alaska, but also four-day party cruises out of Los Angeles. She later carved a niche for herself as a popular fly-cruise and UK-based cruise ship before being withdrawn and scrapped in 1975. The *Chusan* was used solely as a cruise ship from 1969 onwards, but was withdrawn and sold for demolition only four years later. In that brief time she became very popular with the so-called Chusan Club, comprising repeat passengers. The Chusan Club organised a fly-cruise to join the ship at Tenerife on her final inbound voyage returning from South Africa:

> If you are a *Chusan* lover, one who has enjoyed the friendly atmosphere and good service that has been the *Chusan's* hallmark of pleasurable cruising over the years, then you will want to know about this unique chance to sail in her before she leaves the cruising scene. This is a special opportunity offered to past *Chusan* passengers to make one more voyage with her – an opportunity to enjoy a happy and memorable event.

The *Himalaya* was also extensively used as a cruise ship, finishing with a series of cruises from Australia before she was sold for demolition in 1974. The *Arcadia* then took up the role of Australian cruise ship, now a permanent feature within the P&O Cruises portfolio.

The changes made during the career of the *Himalaya* in order to keep her abreast of the market were typical of this generation of P&O and Orient Line vessels. As built, the *Himalaya* could accommodate 770 first- and 390 tourist-class passengers. The main alterations were the fitting of a Thornycroft-type smoke deflector to her funnel in 1951, installation of full air conditioning and anti-roll stabilizers in the late 1950s and early 1960s, and her eventual conversion to a one-class ship for 1,420 passengers in 1963. W. Paul Clegg wrote in an article which first appeared in *Sea Breezes* in August 1974:

> Apart from small alterations, such a the installation of a cinema on the starboard side of the engine casing on the Promenade Deck, only names of rooms have changed, purposes have not. For example,

The *Chusan* (1950) was such a popular cruise ship that she had her own devoted following called 'The Chusan Club'.

the former first-class dining saloon on D Deck forward is now known as the Drake Restaurant, while the former tourist-class dining saloon (aft on the same deck) is now the Tasman Restaurant. The former, a magnificent room extending the full width of the ship, is beautifully furnished with panelling, engraved mirrors and drapery, and recalls the era of 'Port out–Starboard home' in a unique way. Similarly, the former first-class public rooms on the Promenade Deck are strongly reminiscent of the 'old days' which the application of more modern furnishings cannot entirely disguise.

Following a weekend cruise from Southampton to Zeebrugge in May 1974, the twenty-five-year-old *Himalaya* undertook her last liner voyage to Australia. On arrival she undertook a short series of farewell cruises from Sydney and then sailed to the ship breakers' yard.

Shaw Savill put new tonnage into the Australia and New Zealand round-the-world passenger route with the innovative passenger-only *Southern Cross*. The *Southern Cross* was completed by Harland & Wolff in 1955 and had a capacity for 1,100 tourist-class passengers. This configuration was an attempt to make the ship independent of the strike-prone Australian docker in order to allow sailing schedules to be maintained. The *Southern Cross* had traditional steam turbine machinery which was placed aft, leaving additional space for public rooms and open decks amidships, as well as an additional twenty cabins over a conventional ship design. She settled into the round-the-world service and in her first year she also managed to fit in three short Mediterranean cruises.

The *Southern Cross* was joined in 1962 by the near-sister *Northern Star*. This ship, however, had a greater one-class passenger complement of 1,437. Rising operating costs saw the withdrawal of the *Southern Cross* in 1971. The *Southern Cross* had operated some cruises in 1969 and 1970

The *Northern Star* (1962) leaving Southampton on a liner voyage in February 1969.

The forward dining saloon aboard the *Northern Star*'s sister ship, the *Southern Cross*.

between liner voyages, and ended her service under the Red Ensign with four cruises from Liverpool and a final round-the-world voyage. Under the Greek flag, she later returned to the UK cruise market as the *Calypso*, and was broken up as the *Ocean Breeze* as late as 2004. From 1971 the *Northern Star* was increasingly used for cruising, both from the UK and from Australia. By the

The 'Tavern' on the *Southern Cross*.

A typical single berth cabin on the *Southern Cross*.

autumn of 1975, she had become uneconomical to operate and was sold for scrap, just thirteen years after she had been commissioned. The *Northern Star* had, in any case, begun to suffer serious mechanical difficulties when boiler tube failure had embarrassingly terminated a Mediterranean cruise in 1974.

P&O-Orient, now a fully merged entity, introduced its last liner tonnage with the *Oriana*, built in 1960 at a cost of £15 million, and the *Canberra*, which cost £16 million the following year. The engines were placed aft in *Canberra*, as was the case with the Shaw Savill round-the-world liners. The P&O-Orient ships were much bigger, designed for the new transpacific passenger service in which speed and economies of scale were the keynotes. The *Oriana* had accommodation for 638 first- and 1,496 tourist-class passengers, and the *Canberra* 556 first- and 1,616 tourist-class passengers. The initial success of the two liners, however, was rapidly overtaken by air travel and they were transferred to P&O Cruises in 1973.

The *Oriana* was one of the first deep-sea ships to be fitted with bow thruster units to assist manoeuvring in confined spaces, a feature that seems to have been available for a long time but which, in fact, is relatively new. The *Oriana* was perhaps a more formal ship than the *Canberra*, and had a more complex and confusing layout. Passengers could be discovering new areas on the last day of a cruise aboard the *Oriana*, whereas the *Canberra* tended to keep nothing hidden. Many passengers aboard the *Oriana*, for example, never discovered the huge library aft, whilst another feature of the *Oriana* was the gentle movement and groaning that her hardwood panelling made in a heavy sea. She also had the biggest expanse of open deck space of almost any ship afloat.

Both the *Canberra* and the *Oriana* were redesigned as one-class ships with over 1,700 berths, and began a programme of two- to three-week cruises out of Southampton and fly-cruises from the Mediterranean and elsewhere in winter. It was proposed in 1973 that the *Canberra* should be disposed of because of her size and her deep draft which prevented her from entering many cruise ports. Her large passenger capacity was difficult to fill, and she had lost £5 million in her New York cruise programme over the previous two years. Happily, an improvement in the cruise market provided the *Canberra* with a reprieve and she became a dedicated cruise ship at the expense of the smaller and older *Orsova*, which was sold. In any case, the *Orsova* would have needed a lot spent on her to bring her to a satisfactory one-class cruising standard. For example, she still had a number of first-class inside cabins equipped with bunk beds, but no en-suite facilities.

In August 1970 the *Oriana* set off from Southampton on her annual world cruise. Off Fawley it was discovered that a fire had broken out in boiler room lagging, and the ship was towed back to her berth. The 1,500 passengers were provided, free of charge, with shipboard entertainment and shore excursions around Hampshire and to London before the *Oriana* was ready to resume the cruise a fortnight later. This set her owners back £0.5 million, a paltry sum compared with the lost world cruise of the *Aurora* in 2005, which cost Carnival £22 million (see Chapter 12).

In 1976 P&O undertook a total of thirty cruises: *Canberra* did seventeen, *Oriana* eleven and the remainder were undertaken by the *Arcadia*.

The *Canberra* became highly successful in her cruising role. She developed a considerable following and many passengers went back year after year to this same ship. Many commentators reported that towards the end of her career she had become a piece of history, a time capsule from the era of great liner travel. Fares for the *Canberra's* world cruise in 1976 had cost between £993 and £6,450, contrasting with the escalating fares for her final world cruise in 1997, which was a sell-out after just three days with prices between £5,000 and £34,000. The *Canberra*, like the *Queen Elizabeth 2*, had distinguished herself during the Falkland Islands War, and made media headlines when she arrived at Southampton on completion of her last cruise in 30 September 1977.

The *Arcadia* remained on the Australian cruise programme until 1979 when she was replaced by the much more up-market *Sea Princess*, formerly the Swedish-America liner *Kungsholm* (see Chapter 9). When the elderly *Oriana* displaced the *Sea Princess* in 1981 the Australian cruise

Resplendent in cruising white, the *Andes* (1939) sets off for the Mediterranean during summer 1969.

clientele was none too enamoured and accused P&O of providing a second-class service. The rub was that the *Sea Princess* was withdrawn from Australia to service the cruise market in the UK. The *Oriana*, however, remained on the Australian cruise service until 1986, complete with a small contingent of New South Wales Police to maintain order, when she was sold out of the fleet. She suffered as a cruise ship with the capacity for 1,200 passengers, as her public rooms were capable of accommodating only a third of them at any time during evening periods of entertainment. Cheaper, poorer-quality cabins remained popular with the Australians 'who only went in the cabins to sleep anyway'! Unlike the *Canberra* and *Arcadia*, which had South Asian seamen and stewards, the *Oriana* retained an all-British crew to the last. The *Oriana* was used in China in a static role until damaged in high winds and was scrapped in 2005.

The Royal Mail Line's stately *Andes* was trialled as a cruise ship during the summers between 1956 and 1959, when she ran a popular series of cruises to northern capitals, the Mediterranean and even South Africa. In 1960 she was displaced from liner duties and refitted as a permanent cruise ship. Work included the removal of all cargo spaces, a 250-seat cinema built into No.3 hold, rebuilding the accommodation and fitting air conditioning throughout the vessel. She was targeted at the top end of the cruising market, with a crew of 500 tending on the demands of just 480 cruise passengers. The first cruise under her new guise took place in June 1960. She was soon extremely popular, with 60 per cent of her cruise passengers booking repeat holidays, usually to the Mediterranean, northern Europe or the Caribbean. This keen following quickly developed into the 'Andes Cruise Club', assisting passengers with their bookings. Boiler trouble began to cause problems in 1969 and, with a major survey due in 1972, it was decided that the *Andes* could continue no longer. She sailed to the breakers' yard in 1971, much to the anguish of the Andes Cruise Club.

One last ship deserves mention. She was one of the most striking new builds of the 1950s, the Pacific Steam Navigation Company's beautifully proportioned liner *Reina del Mar*, which was delivered by Harland & Wolff at Belfast in 1956. The *Reina del Mar* carried 207 first, 216 cabin and 343 tourist class on the Liverpool-based South America west coast route. She survived on the route until 1963 and was then restyled as a cruise ship with one-class passenger capacity increased by some 300 berths to 1,047, the installation of a permanent cinema, increased open deck space and additional public rooms.

In 1963 a unique co-operative membership company was floated by Max Wilson (who was then only thirty-five years old) as the Travel Savings Association (TSA). Wilson recognised that a number of passenger liners were being deployed away from their intended services, but that there was an untapped market for relatively cheap 'value for money' sea travel and cruises. Holdings in TSA were wholly owned by Travel Savings Limited, which in turn was owned by British & Commonwealth (parent group of the Union-Castle Line), Canadian Pacific, the Pacific Steam Navigation Company and the Max Wilson Organisation.

Four ships were chartered in. They were the *Empress of Britain*, to work out of the UK; *Empress of England*, ostensibly on a five-year charter to work out of South Africa; the elderly P&O liner *Stratheden*; and the *Reina del Mar*, which was then still owned by the Pacific Steam Navigation Company but under Union-Castle Line management. As such she commenced service in June 1964, with her yellow Pacific Steam Navigation Company funnel defaced with the letters TSL in blue and enclosed in a circle. The *Stratheden* completed only four cruises before being sold by P&O. A series of very successful cruises were run by the *Reina del Mar* and the *Empress of England*, which in 1964 included venues such as the New York Trade Fair and the Tokyo Olympics.

The basic TSA idea was that passengers paid instalments to the company and when they had obtained sufficient credit they could book their cruise. Mr Wilson recognised the increasing spending-power of young people and promoted two under-35s cruises in April 1964 using the *Empress of Britain*. For Travel Savings Association members the ten-day cruises to Tangier, Gibraltar and Lisbon cost between £38 and £103. Max Wilson said:

> Young people have not taken to sea cruises because they have the idea that these are for older people and also because they are too expensive. We are a sea-minded nation, and by designing these cruises for under-35s with top-class entertainment and at a price young people can afford, I believe we will attract a vast new market which the shipping industry so badly needs.

The two cruises were under-subscribed. Max Wilson was forty years ahead of the market but was eventually to be proved correct by brands such as Carnival's Ocean Village and German Seetours, which were initiated early in the twenty-first century. The *Empress of Britain* was withdrawn from charter in 1964 and sold to the Greek Line. Although the TSA appeared to be a success, there were clearly problems and it collapsed in 1965 when Max Wilson pulled out of the scheme. The *Empress of England* and *Empress of Canada* reverted to the old routine of summer liner duties and winter cruises, the latter largely from New York to the Caribbean. In their 1968–69 winter refits they received the new green and white CP Ships' livery.

The *Empress of England* was sold to the Shaw Savill Line in January 1970 to become their *Ocean Monarch*. The *Empress of Canada* was sold in 1971 to Carnival Cruise Lines Inc. (see Chapter 11). As the *Ocean Monarch*, Shaw Savill maintained the former *Empress of England* on cruises and occasional liner voyages. After a single round-the-world voyage, Shaw Savill invested £2 million in a twelve-month refit which included structural alterations to provide new public rooms and staterooms at the expense of cargo space. The work was undertaken by Cammell

The inaugural voyage of the *Ocean Monarch* (1957), formerly the *Empress of England*, took place on 11 April 1970 from Liverpool.

Laird at Birkenhead, who reportedly lost over £1 million on the job, having underestimated the amount of work required. The first cruise in her new guise commenced from Southampton on 16 October 1971. However, mechanical trouble brought early retirement and she was sold for demolition in 1974. Passengers already booked on her summer cruise programme were offered alternative cruises on the *Northern Star*.

The *Reina del Mar* eventually became an integral part of the Union-Castle Line fleet, being at first under charter from Pacific Steam; her ownership was later changed to the Royal Mail Line, and in 1973 she was bought by Union-Castle. In this cruising role she could accommodate 980 passengers. One major lesson did come out of the TSA experience – the rapid turnarounds between cruises required the development of containerised and locked bonded stores for rapid loading and unloading, a system widely adopted since by cruise operators and airlines alike.

A promotional article for the *Reina del Mar* in the 1972/73 Union-Castle/Safmarine passenger magazine *Safari* reported:

> She's what I call a 'shippy' ship with wide teak laid decks, wooden handrails, gleaming brass fittings and spotlessly clean throughout. You really feel you are in a ship and not, as is sometimes the case these days, in no more than a modern hotel afloat. There is ample sheltered deck space and plenty of deck chairs for which no charge is made. She has two swimming pools – big by cruise ship standards – and both surrounded by wide lido decks for soaking up the sun. Below decks and the centre of shipboard life is the Coral Lounge, a huge comfortable room which occupies the whole of the forward part of the

The cruise ship *Reina del Mar* (1956) in Union-Castle Line colours at Southampton in 1968.

Promenade Deck and is surely one of the largest public rooms of any ship afloat. In addition there are several other lounges – all with bars; a cinema, library, shops, hairdressing salons, and for the children their own playroom and a playdeck with a paddling pool.

Under Union-Castle colours, the *Reina del Mar* carved herself a valuable niche in the UK and South African cruise markets. In April 1973 a twenty-six-day cruise from Southampton to the Caribbean was advertised at prices from only £265. Her South African cruises to ports in South America were always well patronised. She was withdrawn in 1975, a victim of rising fuel costs which had rendered her uneconomical.

The Union-Castle Line also used the *Stirling Castle* for two farewell cruises at the end of her career. These were from Southampton to Spain and the Mediterranean, after which she was sold for scrap. Near-sister the *Capetown Castle*, which was sold out of the fleet in 1967, offered cruising-style return voyages to South Africa via the Cape Verde Islands during her last few years in service. These were popular with excursion passengers also keen to enjoy the coastal voyage between Capetown and Durban. The passenger mail ship service finally closed in 1977.

The last traditional passenger cargo liner to be built (except for the present *St Helena*, still serving that high-rise island until such time as an international airport can be engineered) was Blue Funnel Line's *Centaur*. She was built as a replacement for the elderly *Charon* and *Gorgon* which maintained the Freemantle to Singapore passenger, sheep and general cargo route which had been operated by Blue Funnel since 1889. Peter Kohler described the ship in an article which first appeared in *Ships Monthly* in May 2007:

People joked that the *Centaur* carried some 4,700 passengers, of whom only 196 were human: her main trade was the transport of 4,500 sheep and 40 dairy cows northbound from Freemantle to Singapore and 700 cattle southbound from Derby and Broome, in North Western Australia, to Freemantle. The *Centaur* also carried general, liquid and refrigerated cargo worked by three deck cranes and, for the

The Blue Funnel Line's *Centaur* (1964) was the last of the traditional passenger and cargo ships to be built for traditional liner service in the 1960s. She is seen here as a new ship at the Princes Landing Stage in Liverpool at the start of her delivery voyage to Australia on 20 January 1964.

The school ship *Devonia* (1939) and formerly the troopship *Devonshire* is seen in the Mersey at the start of a summer cruise in 1967.

The *Nevasa* (1956) was one of the last pair of troopships to be built.

first time on a Blue Funnel ship, power-driven hatch covers. Her one-class accommodation was no less versatile with two luxury suites and ten twin-bedded cabins with private facilities to seventy-seven one-, two- and four-berth cabins, of which two had private facilities.

In the 1970s fly cruises were advertised from the UK and the round trip cruise was marketed locally as 'Pleasure Island *Centaur*'. By all accounts she was a delight to travel on, save for the ever-present scent of farmyards coming from the masthead extractor exhausts. Under certain conditions, as the ship approached Singapore, the smell could be so bad that cruise passengers refrained from taking to the decks until the sheep were off-loaded and the animal pens hosed down. The vessel was flagged out to Singapore in 1973 when she was transferred to an associate company, Eastern Fleet Singapore, and in 1979 Hong Kong and Manila were included in her route, the round trip increasing to twenty-five days. Popular with her human cargo to the last she was withdrawn in 1982 in the face of a new generation of large sheep carriers.

The *Centaur* then deputised for a twelve-month period on the St Helena run between Avonmouth and Cape Town whilst the 1964-built *St Helena* was requisitioned to support the Falkland Islands War. At this stage corrosion from animal urine was beginning to cause severe plating damage, serious decay of parts of the aluminium superstructure had set in and she was suffering mechanical problems. Nevertheless she traded until 1995 under the Chinese flag before succumbing to the breaker's torches.

The second *St Helena*, commissioned in 1990, survives the *Centaur* as Britain's very last passenger cargo liner, and she too offers a variety of cruises and fly cruises while she plies her normal trade. Managed by Andrew Weir the 'RMS', as she is known, can accommodate 104 passengers plus an additional twenty-eight inter-island passengers between Ascension and St Helena. There is a large Promenade Deck with a swimming pool and sun lounge, playroom and quiet lounge. On A Deck is a large observation lounge facing forward, the ship's doctor and launderette and some cabins, although most cabin accommodation is on B and C Decks below. The bureau and shop are on B Deck and the dining room and galley are on C Deck. Normally rostered from the UK to Cape Town the *St Helena* will cease the UK calls in 2008 and will be based in the South Pacific from Cape Town. She remains the last liner.

IN SCHOOL

The troopship *Dunera*, which had been completed in 1937, was converted into a dedicated school ship in 1961, complete with classrooms, dormitories and other teaching facilities, as well as a full-time Director of Studies. This renewed the British India Line's school-ship programme which had been inaugurated in the 1930s (see Chapter 5). The *Dunera* could carry 830 school children (aged twelve years and upwards) as well as adults, and catered for groups of both sexes. There was also excellent accommodation for independent cruise passengers wishing to take advantage of the educational cruise itineraries. The first season of six cruises carried out by the *Dunera* proved so successful that British India promptly purchased her near-sister ship, *Devonshire*, from the Bibby Line as a partner. Under the name *Devonia*, the second school ship was ready for her inaugural cruise out of Liverpool in April 1962.

The success of the school-ship programme released the post-war-built and now redundant troopship *Nevasa* from lay up in 1965 for conversion. The *Nevasa* was considerably bigger than the *Dunera* and *Devonia*, with dormitory accommodation for groups of twelve to forty-two for a maximum of 1,090 children and berths for up to 307 adults, typically about seventy teachers plus independent passengers.

The maiden cruise of the *Nevasa* started from Southampton on 28 October, carrying parties of children and teachers from Staffordshire. The thirteen-day voyage included calls at Madeira, Tangier and Lisbon. Her second cruise started at Southampton, but like so many of these cruises ended in the Mediterranean having visited Malta, Piraeus, Izmir and Itea, this time with parties from West Sussex and the Borough of Barnet.

With three ships in service between 1965 and 1967, some 37,000 children and 10,000 teachers were catered for annually. The ships became familiar sites in the Mersey, the Tyne, the Clyde, Belfast Lough and Tilbury, but in 1967 the *Dunera* was withdrawn from service and sold for demolition, with the *Devonia* following the next year. Their replacement was the former East African mail boat the *Uganda*. The *Uganda* was remodelled with dormitory accommodation for about 900 children, with teachers in three-berth cabins and with a number of additional cabins available for independent passengers.

The school day at sea was broken up into five forty-five-minute periods. These were: 'Assembly Hall', when members of the ship's educational staff would lecture the students on the next port of call, 'Deck Games', and 'Private Study' or 'Classrooms'. Usually three teachers would supervise about forty-five children. Stories of misbehaviour by the students are legendary. For example, there were reports of 'passion patrols' laid on by the ship's crew in order to restrain youthful vigour, and there was an incident when an Arab businessman wanted to buy three sixth-form girls for his harem. A ship-load of school children mixed with independently-booked adult passengers created some interesting sensitivities, and overall discipline needed to be firm, but restrained.

There are numerous stories which have been told about the school ships. One teacher recounts:

As had been expected, the Bay of Biscay lived up to its reputation and the morning after I had the dubious privilege of sitting on the children's recreation deck surrounded by bodies in various degrees of prostration. The navigation notes, which were issued to the children every day to enable them to keep their logs up to date, calmly informed us that the *Uganda* had experienced a Force 8 gale. … and leaving the Canaries the voyage was rather marred by the arrival on board of a mystery bug which laid half the passengers and crew very low for forty-eight hours. The hospital was extremely overworked for a period and several of the dormitories had to be requisitioned as emergency centres.

The English Channel and Tilbury appeared all too quickly and 900 school children disembarked having thoroughly enjoyed a real experience and education. It was education not only in the sense that they had learned much from what they had seen and heard, but that they had learnt much about each other by living together as a community in the unique atmosphere of shipboard life.

The *Nevasa* and *Uganda* continued in service until 'unprecedented increases in operating costs' forced the withdrawal of the *Nevasa* from the school-ship programme at the end of 1974. The *Uganda* continued the programme alone, and in 1976 she visited sixty different ports on twenty-seven cruises, thirteen of which were winter fly-cruises to the Eastern Mediterranean. Yet by the early 1980s the *Uganda* was no longer able to sell all her berths, as the fare for a two-week voyage had risen beyond the means of many parents, even though the demand from adult passengers remained strong. The end came unannounced when the *Uganda* was called up to serve as a hospital ship in the Falkland Islands War in 1982. The children on the last cruise were ordered ashore at Naples and flown home, their holiday peremptorily cut short on the last day of the UK school-ship era.

9
ENTER THE CRUISE SHIP

The cruise ship has become quite a different breed from the passenger liner. The cruise ship carries no cargo and it tends to make a landfall in the early morning for passengers to run ashore ready for an evening departure and another landfall the next morning. This daily routine is based on the premise that two days and more at sea is too long for a cruise ship to entertain its passengers without a port of call. The cruise ship has evolved in a number of other directions. Economies of scale, whereby the more passengers carried per ton of fuel oil, per crew member, per unit capital depreciation, mean that new builds have inevitably got larger. The ships have also become broader in the beam to retain the essential shallow draft for entry to many of the more popular cruise destinations.

From *The Decline and Revival of the British Passenger Fleet*, 2001.

The four-fold increase in fuel oil costs in 1973–74, coupled with rises in crew wages and maintenance and support service costs, systematically put most of the cruise ships converted from liners out of the UK-flagged cruise business. Although this coincided with a significant downturn in cruising by UK holiday makers, it also coincided with an unprecedented number of foreign-flagged vessels plying their trade in the British market (indeed some of these ships were in fact former UK-flagged liners).

Commentary in the August 1974 edition of *Sea Breezes*, reporting the proposed withdrawal of the *Reina del Mar* by the Union-Castle Line, was as follows:

… it is a poor outlook for cruising from British ports under the British flag. There will, within a year or so, probably be a better opportunity for a cruise under the hammer and sickle of the Soviet Union, than under the Red Ensign of Britain, and the Liberian flag ships of the Sitmar Line will also be scooping up the British cruising public.

One of the critical purchases of redundant British tonnage was that by American Ted Arison, in collaboration with the Boston firm American International Travel Service, when he bought the Canadian Pacific liner *Empress of Canada* in 1972. He placed her in the cheap no-frills American cruise ship market as the *Mardi Gras*, under the trading title of Carnival Cruise Lines Inc. Her very first promotional cruise for the travel trade came to grief when she ran aground, but the insurance

The *Canberra* (1961), almost at the end of her career, sails down Southampton Water at the start of a cruise.

pay-out covered the damages plus the original cost of ship purchase. Thereafter, her two-week fun cruises from Miami achieved 95 per cent loadings throughout the first year of operation.

With the collapse of the Greek Line in 1975, Ted Arison was able to buy the *Queen Anna Maria*, none other than the former *Empress of Britain*. She became the first *Carnivale* and was soon joined by the former Union-Castle mail ship *Transvaal Castle* (latterly the *SA Vaal*), which became the cruise ship *Festivale*. In 1978 Mr Arison took delivery of his first purpose-built ship, the *Tropicale*. He was set on becoming the richest man in Florida, with Carnival Cruise Lines eventually to become a key player in the global cruise industry. Today his brands include both the Cunard Line and P&O Cruises, neither of which is now British-owned, although some of their ships remain registered in the UK.

With the disposal of so many UK-flagged former liners following the fuel crisis in 1973–74, only two companies remained in the cruise industry after the 1975 season. These were the two that Carnival would eventually own: Cunard, who offered cruises and occasional liner voyages with the *Queen Elizabeth 2*, and P&O, whose cruise ship and former liners were the *Canberra* and *Oriana*, with the *Arcadia* in Australian waters. Indeed, the very first winter season (1969–70) of the *Queen Elizabeth 2* was spent on cruises from New York to the Caribbean. The only other British cruise ship in operation was the *Uganda*, plying the school-ship trade under the British India Line banner.

A new class of purpose-built cruise ship of relatively modest proportions now emerged. These were the Cunard Line twins *Cunard Adventurer* and *Cunard Ambassador* and P&O's *Spirit of London*, which had joined their owners' cruise operations when they were commissioned between 1971 and 1972. This breed of cruise ship was designed for economy of operation with a relatively

The school ship *Uganda* (1952) seen at the end of a cruise at Southampton in early 1968.

The *Arcadia* (1954) arriving at Southampton with a full complement of cruise passengers.

modest passenger capacity, but with draft and manoeuvrability that allowed access to all but the smallest ports. Both Cunard and P&O had realised that they had been too long in ordering dedicated cruise tonnage and both had bought into existing orders during construction. The first, the *Cunard Adventurer*, was ordered in the first instance by Overseas National Airways, an

The *Queen Elizabeth* 2 (1969) passing down Southampton Water off Hythe at the start of a summer cruise in 2001.

American airline, and completed under the new ownership of Cunard-ONA Limited, and the second was the *Spirit of London*, ordered originally as one of a pair by Lauritz Kloster but delivered to P&O Cruises.

The *Cunard Adventurer* had a passenger capacity of 806 in thirty-one outside 'deluxe' double cabins, 178 outside doubles, 104 inside doubles and four single cabins. There was a swimming pool, a lido deck, restaurant, lounge, night club (the 329 Club, named after the builders' yard number for the ship, a precedent set by the *Queen Elizabeth 2*), six bars, a hairdressing salon, sauna and massage rooms, shops, cinema and the Sky Room Bar, which provided an impressive panoramic view from above the wheelhouse. The *Cunard Adventurer* had a capacity of only 14,151 gross tons, and was equipped with four diesel engines which could maintain a service speed of 21 knots, or slower speeds for lower fuel consumption. Her initial cruise set off in November 1971, taking passengers to the Caribbean. Unhappily she suffered serious mechanical failure in the Bay of Biscay, where she was without power for four hours, and had to wait at Lisbon for replacement housing for the starboard propeller shaft. Her sister, the *Cunard Ambassador*, was commissioned for the same consortium a year later in 1972.

The two ships became wholly Cunard-owned when Overseas National Airways withdrew from the partnership. The ships never carried the Cunard funnel colours, sporting an all-white funnel just as the *Queen Elizabeth 2* had done until she returned from the Falkland Islands War in 1983. The *Cunard Adventurer* and *Cunard Ambassador* rarely strayed from the Caribbean, offering seven-day fly-cruises from the United States and the UK, starting and ending at San Juan in Puerto Rico. They also ran occasional cruises from Port Everglades and between New York and Bermuda.

The *Cunard Ambassador* (1972) saw barely two years' service as a cruise ship.

Just how successful they were is unclear, but plans were in hand to replace them just as soon as they had been commissioned.

Both ships suffered engine-room fires. The *Cunard Adventurer* was disabled in July 1974, although she was soon repaired and back in service. Just two months later, a crippling engine-room fire aboard the *Cunard Ambassador* caused her to be abandoned whilst she was on an empty positioning-run between Port Everglades and New Orleans. All the crew of 240 were taken off safely. The ship was later towed to a safe anchorage and declared beyond repair. Rebuilt as a livestock carrier, she suffered a second engine-room fire in 1984, after which her owners sold the ship for demolition. The *Cunard Adventurer* remained in the Cunard fleet only until 1976, the ship having suffered further mechanical problems the previous year.

The new P&O cruise ship *Spirit of London* arrived at Southampton on 17 October 1972 for her maiden voyage – a delivery passage to San Juan. During the traditional open day ceremonies she was described by a director of P&O as the first of 'our second tier passenger fleet of small purpose-built cruise ships, designed to retain P&O's world leadership in cruising right through the 1980s'. Her initial voyage permitted 180 berths to be sold in the UK, whilst the remaining 550 were sold on the American market. From San Juan the *Spirit of London* went on to Los Angeles to commence a programme of short cruises to Mexico in winter and Alaska in summer. Although targeted at the American market, fly-cruise tickets from the UK were available for about £500 per head. All 409 cabins were equipped with toilets, baths or showers, a radio and a telephone, with the focus on top-class entertainment and first-class hotel accommodation.

The new-generation P&O cruise ship was a considerable success on the West Coast but her owners were frustrated that a consort could neither be bought off the shelf nor bespoke-tailored in time to harvest the rich pickings then on offer. So it was that P&O acquired the thriving Seattle-based Princess Cruises in 1974, and the *Spirit of London* was transferred to that operator, but retaining British registry, as the *Sun Princess* (see Chapter 10).

The new P&O cruise ship *Spirit of London* (1972), better remembered as the *Sun Princess*.

The second generation of cruise ships for the Cunard Line were the successors to the small *Cunard Ambassador* twins, the *Cunard Countess* and *Cunard Princess*. The latter was launched as the *Cunard Conquest*, but her name was changed before delivery. They were larger ships than the earlier pair, and had a gross tonnage of 17,586. The *Cunard Countess* left Burmeister & Wain's yard at Copenhagen, after her launch in September 1974 for fitting-out in Italy, arriving on station at San Juan in August 1976. Four British shipyards had declined to respond to invitations to tender for the job when they were issued in November 1972; British yards were already the poor neighbours of the up-and-coming continental yards for passenger shipbuilding. The younger sister, the *Cunard Countess*, was commissioned the following year.

The pair commenced a series of week-long cruises in the Caribbean, with alternate itineraries every week, so that passengers could opt for seven nights or fourteen nights at sea, plus combinations ashore in Puerto Rico before flying home. In the off-season one ship transferred to the West Coast of America for cruises from San Fransisco and Vancouver. It was about this time that many operators realised that top-quality accommodation was not enough, but first-class entertainment needed to be provided to attract passengers as well.

The *Cunard Countess* and *Cunard Princess* were initially highly profitable for their owners and very popular with their clientele. The ships had eight passenger decks and had berths for 750 passengers in 373 cabins. They featured a panoramic observation lounge above the bridge, a night club/cinema, a casino and a 371-seat restaurant, in addition to the ship's shop and hairdressing salon, an activities room which doubled as a conference room, a children's room which could also be used as a private dining room, and no less than seven bars. With the funnel placed well aft, there were large open deck areas as well as a heated open-air swimming pool just forward of the funnel on the lido deck.

The profitability of the ships waned in the late 1970s as operating costs increased. In October 1980 Cunard made a bid to reduce costs by announcing that the two ships would be transferred

The *Cunard Countess* (1976) approaching the quay stern first at Road Town, British Virgin Isles, on the weekly circuit from San Juan.

to the Bahamian flag and the British crew replaced with a locally recruited crew. On hearing this news, the crew of the *Cunard Countess* immediately immobilised the ship when she docked next, as it happened, at Bridgetown in Barbados. Stranded passengers were flown back to San Juan to await connecting flights home and the vessel's next cruise was cancelled. In the end there was a good old British compromise. The *Cunard Princess* was registered in Nassau in October 1980, but the *Cunard Countess* was allowed to retain her British registry and many of her crew. Notwithstanding, the two ships soon became a drain on company profits.

The Falkland Islands War saw the *Cunard Countess* more profitably employed, under charter to the Ministry of Defence, to operate a ferry service between Ascension Island and the Falklands. Returning to civilian duties she rejoined her partner at San Juan before the *Cunard Princess* initiated a programme of Mediterranean-based cruises. In December 1990, the *Cunard Princess* became a 'rest and recuperation' centre for American military personnel then stationed in the Middle East during the Gulf War. American troops boarded their stationary three-day cruise in batches of 900, and were treated to every amenity on the ship apart from the casino. This American military charter lasted nine months, complete with machine guns on the bridge wings, after which the ship returned to civilian duties in the Mediterranean. The two sisters were sold in 1995 and 1996 respectively.

In 1978 P&O bought the *Sea Princess* on the second-hand market in order to develop its position in the UK cruise market. She had been built by John Brown & Company on the Clyde as the *Kungsholm* for the Swedish America Line in 1966, and was designed with the dual role of North Atlantic liner and New York-based cruise ship. She had also later served under the Bermudan and Liberian flags. P&O sent her to Germany for an extensive refit, during which her forward funnel and mainmast were removed and the remaining aft funnel extended in height.

The *Sea Princess* (1966) carrying bunting thrown over the side on departure from Southampton in 1985.

Her accommodation and public rooms were kept pretty much intact and even the paintings hung in the public rooms remained as before. The passenger capacity was increased to 840 in 400 cabins. A second outside swimming pool was built on the Promenade Deck beside the new Carousel Lounge, the latter a lido bar by day and discotheque at night.

The *Sea Princess* was dispatched to Sydney in March 1979 to take over the Australian cruise programme from the obsolescent *Arcadia*. The new ship heralded heights of luxury never before enjoyed by Australian cruise passengers, and this became the advertising theme for the ship. Her British crew was rostered for four months' duty with two months off for the officers and just one month off for other ranks. Most of the seamen and engine-room staff were Pakistani, and there were Goanese dining-room stewards and the obligatory Chinese laundry.

An article by I. Mackay which first appeared in *Sea Breezes* in January 1982 reported:

> Along with the tickets and labels there is a small card headed 'P&O Cruises - Restaurant Seating'. This looks harmless on the front side with the times given for breakfast, luncheon and dinner, but when the card is reversed, the voyager is required to state name, age, cabin and berth number, sitting desired and lastly age group with whom you wish to be seated – under 30 or over 30 – please tick box! The card had to be dispatched at once to the company.

How do P&O arrive at 30? It seems clear that those over 30 are among the elderly, the decrepit and those under that fanciful age are the youthful, the inheritors! I cheated and did not return the card. However, the system was equal to this infringement; the head waiter placed me between two ladies, one a sprightly 80-year-old from Auckland called Elsie and the other a young blonde Australian named Carol.

Mr Mackay goes on to report an enjoyable cruise on a wonderful if rather impersonal ship. He also describes the feeling of well-being that there is on a cruise ship, where only good news is reported in the daily edition of the *Princess Patter*, with only good things to enjoy on board and ashore, the ship being protected from the everyday stresses of the world beyond.

The luxury ship was transferred to the lucrative Mediterranean cruise market in 1981. The old *Oriana* was sent out to the Antipodes (see Chapter 8) and P&O had a hard time explaining why the Australian cruise market should make do with such former glory at the expense of their recent comparative luxury.

THE ENTERTAINER

By Joan Butler (viola)

Fiddlers' pay is legendarily meagre. The wage earned by a string quartet on the *Canberra* in that great ship's twilight years was even less than might have been earned at home on the freelance circuit. Still, there were compensations. The exotic destinations, yes, although there was never enough time to spend ashore and explore them. But it was the lifestyle, one to which we could never otherwise aspire, that made those cruises so unforgettable.

From the very first day on board, the three-tier class system was apparent. Top passengers, bottom crew; and in the middle the entertainers, the dancers, singers, bands, comedian, magician, string quartet, all with the obligations of an employee but the privileges of a passenger. The obligations were never too demanding and the privileges were considerable, in some cases even exceeding those of the passengers. Greater concessions on the already duty-free goods, cut-price shore excursions should we wish to go on them.

The rooms where the entertainments took place were not designed with acoustics in mind. The bands and singers had the benefit of amplification, but we had to do battle with the deadening effects of soft furnishings and thick carpets. Nonetheless, we acquired a small and loyal following who, not only attended our every concert, but spread the word into the bargain, and our audience swelled gratifyingly. We gave them a potpourri drawn from the classical repertoire, arrangements of timeless ballads, witty up-tempo numbers and, woven into every programme, the underlying thread of all cruising romance. Among our regulars was a charming couple, probably in their fifties, cultured, friendly and un-ostentatiously well-heeled, who had met on the ship during a world cruise the previous year, fallen in love and, quite simply, stayed on board. They kept the same first-class suite from cruise to cruise and had made no plans to return to dry land and reality.

Unfortunately we never saw at any of our concerts that hard-core of every passenger list, the eye-popping bevy of ageing, ripsaw-voiced, brass blondes, bedecked with gold chains and jewels, who left no doubt as to their chief reason for being on the cruise. Rumour generally had it that they were the womenfolk of those hardworking fellows who had made the foolish mistake of getting caught, and who were now languishing at Her Majesty's pleasure while the fruits of their labours were being single-mindedly squandered. We idly wondered what they would have made of a string quartet.

Towards the end of each cruise there was always one unscheduled show. All the entertainers got together and put on a grand evening below decks for the crew. The descent to crew quarters brought home the big divide between the extremities of cruising's social scale. Here were no luxury lounges, exquisitely fitted dining rooms, low lights and plush upholstery. Those spartan lower decks had all the austerity of 'downstairs', in that well-known television serial.

On our first cruise the crew was unsure what to expect from a string quartet. Something prim and straight-laced, possibly. We went into 'Star Wars' with all guns blazing, followed it with 'Those Were the Days' and 'Viva Espana', by which time surprise had given way to cheers and singing loud enough to be heard on the Sun Deck.

Being a quartet offering a wide variety of musical styles, we had devised for ourselves a selection of names, each time choosing the one most suitable to the occasion. Later that year, as we were giving a recital in Birmingham, (playing, as befitted the programme, under one of our more classically oriented names) we were aware of a whispering in the audience. All was made clear afterwards, as we were surrounded and plied with questions and compliments. A couple in the audience had been on one of our cruises, and had recognised us. We had played on the *Canberra* – we were famous!

10

THE PRINCESS AND
THE P&O

In 1965 Princess Cruises was founded by Seattle businessman Stanley MacDonald, and undertook its inaugural series of cruises by chartering the handsome two-funnelled Canadian Pacific Railway steamer *Princess Patricia*. She had been built in 1949 by Fairfields at Govan, with high-class overnight accommodation for the Vancouver–Victoria–Seattle service. Cruises from Los Angeles to Mexico and in due course to Alaska were decidedly new territory for what was a conventional Canadian coastal steamer. Perhaps surprisingly, the *Princess Patricia* was an immediate success in her new role, so much so that the brand new Italian ship *Italia* was taken on charter ready for the 1967 season and given the name *Princess Italia*. The chartered *Princess Carla* joined the fleet in 1968, and the Norwegian cruise ship *Island Venture* was chartered in 1971 before she had even been completed, and was given the new name *Island Princess*.

The *Island Venture* and sister *Sea Venture* were ordered by Norwegian Cruiseships A/S of Oslo for the New York to Caribbean cruise market. Equipped with 324 cabins, including forty-seven described as deluxe, they had a passenger capacity of 749. The ships required a crew of 301, of which 265 were employed on hotel duties. There were two large lounges, a multi-purpose theatre, four dance floors and three bars on the lounge deck, plus two heated swimming pools – one aft on the lounge deck, the other on the sun deck complete with a sliding glass roof. One unusual feature was that the ship's kitchens were entirely lined with stainless steel.

By the early 1970s Princess Cruises of Seattle had become an important West Coast Pacific cruise operator with a fleet of largely new ships. All the ships were on charter, and Princess Cruises found that, despite excellent marketing and delivery, they were sorely under-capitalised. Meanwhile P&O had commissioned the *Spirit of London* but was unable to order or buy additional coverage quickly enough to satisfy the acknowledged business prospects then developing in the United States. The financial and business support of the mighty P&O Group was clearly as attractive to Princess Cruises, as the cruise ships held by Princess were to P&O.

The deal was struck and Princess Cruises became a P&O subsidiary, with its headquarters in Los Angeles. The *Island Princess* was bought outright along with her Norwegian sister the *Sea Venture*, which was renamed the *Pacific Princess*. In addition, P&O transferred the *Spirit of London* into the fleet to become the *Sun Princess*. The charter of the *Carla* and *Italia* was terminated. The three Princesses were all registered at London and given British Officers and senior catering staff.

The little coastal steamer *Princess Patricia* (1949) was chartered from Canadian Pacific to initiate Princess Cruises' first cruise programme. (Richard Danielson collection)

The *Island Princess* (1972) leaving Southampton in summer 1996.

The *Pacific Princess* (1971) setting out on a cruise from Tilbury in 1987, offering an almost identical stern quarter profile to her sister ship.

A rather crafty bit of P&O marketing took place in the mid-1970s when the American television series 'The Love Boat' was shot on board the company's ships. The pilot film was made aboard the *Sun Princess*, but later episodes featured the sisters *Pacific Princess* and *Island Princess*. This free covert advertising even attracted a fee from the film company for the free run of the ships. Not only did it benefit sales for Princess Cruises, but it also presented the modern cruising industry in an attractive light, with Captain Stubbing and his thespian crew primarily employed to deal with the romantic entanglements of the passengers.

The first new-building for the P&O subsidiary was completed in 1984 when Princess Diana named the newly delivered *Royal Princess* at Southampton. This was a truly innovative cruise ship featuring an all-outside cabin configuration for the 1,200 passengers with 152 staterooms on decks 7 and 8, all with their own private veranda deck space. The ship set the highest standards of comfort and elegance. The *Royal Princess* cost $150 million, and was set to recover her costs and bring home the dollars.

The *Royal Princess* (now the Bermudan-registered *Artemis* under the P&O Cruises banner) is designed around the concept of a top-calibre international hotel. There are eight passenger decks, with the main public rooms on deck 3, the Riviera Deck, and deck 2, the Plaza Deck. The central and impressive plaza is two decks high. The Continental Dining Room seats 616 on two levels, and the International Lounge on the Riviera Deck, featuring top-class Broadway acts, seats 612. The sun and lido decks offer an array of swimming pools, lounges and cafes, and there is also the obligatory nightclub, casino and health club.

The maiden voyage of the *Royal Princess* was from Southampton to Miami. In mid-Atlantic the ship encountered gale-force winds and high seas. All over the ship, even low down on Dolphin Deck near the water-line, was evidence of damage, including scattered tableware, and there was even a dislodged tree in one of the public rooms. One passenger remarked:

The *Royal Princess* (1984) seen at Southampton in June 2004.

> High out of the water she is a snappy roller, but more disconcerting is her violent pitching. She
> see-saws her way through even the slightest seas. Talking to one of her officers I was told she wasn't
> designed for bad weather, rather a peculiar point to make about a 45,000-ton ship, I thought.

This propensity to roll and pitch in heavy seas is not unique to the *Royal Princess* but is an
affliction of many of the modern high-rise cruise ships. Whilst happy in the blue idyll of the
Caribbean and Mediterranean, they are difficult ships to handle in rough weather. That being so,
reports in later years of the *Royal Princess* rounding Cape Horn in rough weather describe a gentle,
almost soporific, pitching motion. However, some of the young Atlantic waves whipped up in a
storm have an uncomfortable rising shape quite unlike waves in any other ocean.

In 1985 the *Sea Princess* (see Chapter 9) was transferred from P&O Cruises' UK base to the
Princess brand. Even so, Princess remained short of capacity for the business then on offer,
principally from the United States, but also increasingly from Europe. Princess Cruises was able to
purchase the Italian-owned, but Los Angeles-based, Sitmar Cruises in 1988, along with their three
elderly steamships and one new cruise ship, which was also equipped with steam turbine engines.
More importantly Sitmar had outstanding orders for a number of additional new-builds, so that
three new 70,000-ton cruise ships would join the combined fleet over the next five years.

The first of the new builds was the *Sitmar Fairmajesty*, which was delivered in the spring of 1989 as
the *Star Princess* and flagged out to the Liberian registry. She has all the features expected of a modern
cruise ship including a central sweeping circular staircase that dominates the three-deck plaza. On
the lower level are the main lobby, reception area and a patisserie, and the upper levels (the Emerald
and Promenade decks) contain the Galleria shopping arcade and wine bar. She has 735 twin-berth
cabins, fourteen suites and thirty-six mini-suites with outdoor terraces. 510 of the cabins have outside
picture windows, and there are only 165 inside cabins. Ten of the cabins are wheelchair-accessible.

The former troopship *Oxfordshire* (1956) was only displaced as the P&O–Sitmar dedicated Australian cruise ship *Fairstar* in 1997. (John Clarkson)

The two-level Starlight Show Lounge can seat 708 passengers, and the Fountain Court dining room seats 801 on multi-levels making full use of sea views through large windows. The *Star Princess* has a draft of 7.7m which is modest given her massive registered gross tonnage of 62,500.

With the arrival of the *Star Princess*, the stop-gap *Sea Princess* was returned to P&O Cruises and renamed the *Victoria*. (The owners of a Felixstowe-based tug with the name *Victoria* very kindly gave P&O the name and renamed their tug *Oakley*.) Sitmar's new ships now outmoded the small *Sun Princess* and she was sold for further trading in 1989. The older former Sitmar ships were the *Fairsea* and *Fairwind*, which were originally the Cunard Line's *Carinthia* and *Sylvania* (see Chapter 8), and the *Fairstar* which was formerly the Bibby Line troopship *Oxfordshire*. These too were soon disposed of, although the *Fairstar* was retained under P&O Sitmar as the Australia cruise ship until 1997, when she was displaced by the *Fair Princess*, ex-*Fairsea*.

In the early 1980s Trafalgar House, who had bought Cunard in 1971, were looking enviously at P&O. They had acquired 5 per cent of P&O's shares by 1983, and a slanging match ensued between the two companies, during which Cunard was described by P&O as 'messing about in boats'. P&O, however, went on from strength to strength and the Princess cruise fleet stood at sixteen ships by 1994, carrying 430,000 cruise passengers to 250 ports in 100 different countries.

During the 1990s Princess Cruises enlarged its market share and developed its own class of large luxurious cruise ships. It staked its reputation on providing ships with a large number of cabin balconies, high standards of onboard entertainment and good food. The company also prides itself on the extras that include bath robes, flowers and fresh fruit in every cabin. The international flavour of its operations, particularly the American, Canadian and Anglo-Italian influences, are reflected in the current staffing of the ships themselves.

In 1994 all members of the fleet were equipped with aircraft-style black boxes or Voyage Event Recorders. The black boxes continuously record radar, gyro heading, position, speed and date and time.

Only one of the ex-Sitmar ships was originally registered in London. This was the steam turbine-driven *Sky Princess*, which was completed in 1984 as the *Fairsky* for the Sitmar Line, and had been that company's flagship when Princess Cruises took them over. The ship never featured in either UK- or Mediterranean-based cruising, although she proudly carried her port of registry as London. As such she was the last steam turbine-powered passenger vessel to fly the Red Ensign. Much of her time was spent on Alaskan cruises until she became the regular Far Eastern cruise ship in 1999, and was transferred temporarily to Liberian registry. In 2000 she replaced the forty-five-year-old *Fair Princess* from Australia, becoming the *Pacific Sky* for P&O Cruises Australia. Reverting once more to the British register, she was soon flagged out again. In 2005 she was joined by the *Pacific Sun*, formerly in the Carnival Cruise Lines fleet as the *Jubilee*.

The former Sitmar fleet retained Italian crews and Italian registry, although all but the *Island Princess*, *Pacific Princess* and *Royal Princess* were registered in Liberia in the 1990s in order to attract tax benefits. When the *Ocean Princess* was delivered by Fincantieri Catieri Navali Italiani for a price believed to be greater than $300 million in February 2000, she was transferred to UK registry before her maiden voyage. This re-flagging was followed shortly afterwards by the previously Liberian-registered *Sun Princess* and *Sea Princess* (see Chapter 11). By May the *Dawn Princess* and *Regal Princess* were also under the Red Ensign.

Transfer of these five large and modern cruise ships to the UK registry reflected both the high standards maintained by Princess Cruises and the de-merger of parent Group P&O in October 2000 to create the new UK-based parent company of P&O Cruises. Displaced by the larger new tonnage, the now diminutive *Island Princess* left the fleet in the summer of 1999, joining the South Korean Hyundai Group as the *Hyundai Pungak-Ho*. The *Pacific Princess* continued in service a little longer under the marketing strategy 'small and friendly', but she too was sold in 2002.

The *Star Princess* was transferred in 1997 to the P&O Cruises UK-based fleet as a direct replacement for the *Canberra*, renamed *Arcadia* and re-registered in London. The elderly, if not venerable, *Canberra* was then sold for demolition amid cries that she be saved as a preservation project like the old *Queen Mary*. The newly named *Arcadia* received many artefacts and adornments from the *Canberra* when she took up service from the UK, joining the brand new *Oriana* and the *Sea Princess*.

The *Oriana* had been delivered by her German shipbuilders ready for her official naming ceremony by Her Majesty the Queen on 6 March 1995 at Southampton. The ship has a gross tonnage of 69,153 but her draft is only 7.9m. The *Oriana* has twin rudders, three bow thruster units and one thruster unit at the stern, is highly manoeuvrable and is capable of an impressive 24 knots. In many ways she succeeds the *Canberra*, and care was taken to design the ship using an elegant, yet traditional, style that would attract former *Canberra* cruise passengers to the new ship.

The *Oriana* has ten passenger decks, with the teak decking of the Promenade Deck housing the main entertainment areas. The Theatre Royal seats up to 650, and has both an orchestra pit and a revolving stage. There is a four-deck-high marble-clad atrium complete with a full-height waterfall, an oak-panelled lounge bar called Andersons, a casino, the Lord's Tavern pub, Harlequin's multi-purpose dance/disco/nightclub area, and the Pacific Lounge.

'D' deck, above the main Promenade Deck, offers children's facilities, a 200-seat cinema, quiet lounge and library. The engines are set three-quarters aft, and the deck area is consequently very spacious. There are two swimming pools, one 14m long, and the Oasis Health Spa and Conservatory Café. The main restaurants are down below on 'E' deck with the Peninsular Restaurant amidships and the Oriental Restaurant aft, the latter complete with a 17m-long mural

The *Arcadia* (1989) is seen in Southampton Water off Hythe in June 2001.

The *Oriana* (1995) at the start of another cruise from Southampton.

of the Story of Odysseus. There are 3,000 paintings adorning the bulkheads and a magnificent embroidery called 'Glimpses of India', which hangs in the Curzon Room.

The *Oriana* has eight suites, sixteen deluxe staterooms and ninety-four other staterooms on B deck, plus 590 two-bed cabins (some with additional Pullman berths) on decks A to F. There is also a selection of one-, three- and some four-berth cabins. All are well appointed and self contained. Her maiden voyage took her passengers to the Atlantic Isles for twelve nights, with fares starting at £1,199.

The 1990s saw British holidaymakers return to cruising in droves. In 2000 some 800,000 cruise berths were sold in the UK (not necessarily in British-flagged vessels), a figure that was nearly four times greater than that for the early 1990s.

CLYDE–BUILT

So many of the great passenger liners and cruise ships came originally from the Clyde. The Clyde had been the home of the first commercially successful steamship, Henry Bell's little paddle steamer *Comet* of 1812, and the Clyde had fostered maritime engineering and ship building thereafter, until at its peak one in three of the world's ships were Clyde-built. Today there are only three shipbuilding and ship repair yards left.

Perhaps the most famous yard of all was John Brown's at Clydebank. Work on ship number 534 had ceased at the height of the Depression in December 1931, only to resume in April 1934 with Government loans available, conditional on the amalgamation of the Cunard Line and the White Star Line. Number 534 finally slid down the ways in September 1934 proudly carrying the name of her sponsor, Queen Mary. The *Queen Mary* was followed into the Clyde almost exactly four years later by the *Queen Elizabeth*, and together the two Clyde-built Queens were set to rule the Atlantic. War, of course intervened, and it was only after long service as fast and very high capacity troopships that the two super liners were able to ply their intended trade.

After the war the magnificent *Caronia* came also from John Brown's yard. None of the craftsmanship and skills had been lost during the war years and the *Caronia* was a ship designed for the height of luxury and aimed at the deluxe end of the American transatlantic and cruise markets. Other Clyde shipbuilders enjoyed a post-war boom: Alexander Stephen & Sons, Fairfield Shipbuilding & Engineering Company and Barclay, Curle & Company all completed major passenger ship orders in the 1950s.

John Brown continued unabated with a succession of major post-war builds. These included the *Arcadia* for P&O and the Saxonia-quartet for Cunard. The last major passenger liner built at the yard (which had become Upper Clyde Shipbuilders) was the *Queen Elizabeth 2*. In addition the Swedish America Lines' Kungsholm had been delivered from Govan in 1966, later destined to become the *Sea Princess* and P&O Cruises' *Victoria*.

The march of globalisation meant that passenger shipbuilding was becoming cheaper and more economical away from the traditional centres. So it was that the last major passenger unit was delivered from Govan in 1985, the ferry *Norsea*, for service between Hull and Rotterdam. Since then a handful of smaller units have been built for service with Caledonian MacBrayne and other ferry companies, but the tradition of building and fitting out luxury liners and cruise ships has gone forever. Meanwhile, the same pattern of decline has taken place at Newcastle, Belfast, Barrow and Birkenhead.

11

BIG IS BEST BUT SMALL IS SCOTTISH

To this day the *Hebridean Princess* graces the Western Isles with a characteristic leisurely pace as she sails across calm summer waters to a quiet overnight anchorage. She makes occasional longer forays to Ireland, around Britain and even to Scandinavia and Iceland, but most of the more distant destinations fall to her international consort the *Hebridean Spirit*, formerly the small cruise ship *Megaster Capricorn*. Cruising in the Western Isles is now also supported by Noble Caledonia with the tiny *Lord of the Glens*.

From The Kingdom of MacBrayne, 2006.

Cunard, which had been owned by Trafalgar House Investments since 1971, was bought by the construction, engineering and shipbuilding firm Kvaerner in 1996. Cunard, its ships and its brand name, was then resold in 1998 to the now mighty Carnival Corporation of Miami for $500 million. Carnival, of course, had grown from humble beginnings, starting in 1972 with the purchase of the Canadian Pacific Line's *Empress of Canada* (see Chapter 9). During 2002, P&O Cruises planned to merge with Royal Caribbean Cruises, but a counter bid for P&O Princess by the Carnival Corporation led to the merger being abandoned, and in 2003 P&O Cruises became part of Carnival. P&O Cruises included Princess Cruises, Swan Hellenic, P&O Australia, along with Aida (formerly Deutsche Seetouristik) and A'Rosa, both from the German market. Former rivals Cunard and P&O Cruises now found themselves as sister brands in an American-owned organisation, albeit mostly with UK-registered ships.

After her charter as a troop transport in the Falkland Islands War, the *Queen Elizabeth 2* underwent a £10 million refit. She emerged with a pale grey hull and, at last, the Cunard funnel colours instead of the all-white funnel she had previously worn. She sailed for New York in August 1983 and prices for the single trip ranged up to £2,500. In 1987 the *Queen Elizabeth 2* had her turbine engines replaced by a new set of diesel electric machinery, claimed at the time to offer a 50 per cent cut in fuel consumption. Outwardly the only change was a slightly enlarged funnel top to accommodate the exhaust pipes from the nine diesel units. Changes were also made to some of the public rooms, and it was at this time that the ship's main restaurant became the Mauretania Room.

The *Queen Elizabeth 2* on a Norwegian cruise, summer 2007. (Richard Danielson)

In 1999 the Cunard Line refurbished its foreign-registered cruise ship *Caronia* (formerly the *Vistafjord*) and re-registered her at Southampton for use in the UK cruise market. Built by Swan Hunter Shipbuilders Limited at Wallsend in 1973 as a luxury cruise ship and liner for the Norwegian America Line, she was sold along with her elder sister *Sagafjord* to Norwegian American Cruises in 1980. In 1983 the pair were resold to the Cunard Line, and registered in the Bahamas. The *Sagafjord* had since moved on for further service, but the newly renamed *Caronia* represented the height of Cunard luxury. Her public rooms were described as gracious. For example, the split-level Garden Lounge is romantically described in the marketing literature as being 'bathed in natural light by day with a warm glow at night'. The ship retained the traditional lines expected of a passenger liner, and seven circuits of the teak decks of her Promenade Deck amount to one nautical mile. She was eventually sold in 2005 for use by SAGA Cruises under the name *Saga Ruby* and registered at London, joining her former sister the *Vistafjord*, now the foreign-registered *Saga Rose*.

The new *Queen Mary 2* arrived under the Cunard brand at her home port for the first time on Boxing Day 2003. Built at a cost of £550 million by Chantiers Atlantique, St Nazaire, her completion had been marred by a fatal accident when a gangway collapsed whilst shipyard craftsmen and their families were being honoured with an open day. Nonetheless, she completed her sea trials on time and was berthed at Southampton on 8 January 2004, the focus of national attention, ready for her naming ceremony with Her Majesty Queen Elizabeth II presiding. The Queen and the Duke of Edinburgh were escorted by Commodore Ronald Warwick, the ship's

The *Caronia* (1973) leaving Southampton at the start of a cruise on 30 June 2001.

master, and Cunard President Pamela Conover on a tour of the ship. Pamela Conover stated in her welcoming speech:

> *Queen Mary 2* is a transatlantic liner with all the dignity and grace of the liners of the past, she is also a transatlantic liner of the future with both comforts and technology undreamed of when the *Queen Elizabeth 2* was launched. The *Queen Mary 2* heralds the new golden age and represents the triumph of great tradition.

Alas, some commentators cried, 'Bah Humbug! The *Queen Mary 2* is just another gigantic floating block of high rise flats with the aesthetic appeal of a shoe box,' but didn't they say that also of what we now describe as the 'beautiful and sleek' lines of the *Queen Elizabeth 2* when she was new? Claimed as a transatlantic liner, the *Queen Mary 2* is, in truth, yet another cruise ship but one which will be required also to offer timely cruises that start and finish at different ends of the Pond.

Her inaugural voyage from Southampton to Fort Lauderdale via the Canaries and Jamaica was a sell-out. With 2,620 berths and over 1,300 cabins, she will need to maintain near capacity bookings to be profitable. Carnival are playing on the transatlantic liner theme both through the Cunard brand name and by featuring classic liner style interiors such as the Britannia Restaurant, which features two levels, a glass-domed roof and ornamental pillars.

The much-heralded new technology is impressive. She has four electric azimuth pods, two fixed and two directional at her stern, each weighing 250 tons. These, coupled with bow thruster units, enable her to berth in all but the most adverse conditions unaided by tugs, the more remarkable given the size of the ship at 148,528 tons gross. However, size is also a handicap, as many of the smaller cruise venues will have to be served by tender rather than by the ship coming alongside.

The *Aurora* (2000) arriving at Southampton for the first time on 16 April 2000.

New-building for the P&O fleet is the *Aurora*, completed in 2000 as a development of the *Oriana* design, for use in the UK cruise market. The ship is some 76,000 tons gross with a relatively shallow draft of only 7.9m, and has a service speed of 24 knots. The new *Aurora* features four decks of cabins with private deck space, and there is a swimming pool with a retractable megadrome roof. In all, 1,975 passengers can be accommodated in 934 cabins. Alas, during her naming ceremony the bottle of Australian wine failed to smash on impact with the ship's side and several commentators mumbled the words 'Bad luck'!

Meanwhile Princess Cruises had taken delivery of a succession of large ships of the Grand Princess class, each of 109,000 tons gross. Starting with the *Grand Princess* in 1997, the next was the *Golden Princess* in 2001 and *Star Princess* in 2002. The 77,000 tons gross Sun Princess-class included the *Dawn Princess* and *Sea Princess*, all built between 1996 and 1998, and the *Ocean Princess* delivered in 2000. In 2003 and 2004 two 91,000-ton sisters and two 113,000-ton sisters joined the fleet. Of these, only the 77,000 tonners adopted London as their port of registry, the larger ships going to flags which offered better tax concessions to their owners.

The mighty Carnival Corporation has made good use of its many brands, ensuring that they are not in head-on competition. Carnival has also recognised the flexibility that its corporate size allows, and in 2003 both the *Ocean Princess* and *Sea Princess* moved to the UK market as P&O's *Oceana* and *Adonia* respectively. The *Oceana* was marketed as a family ship whereas the *Adonia* was strictly adults only.

The new ships allowed the *Arcadia* (ex-*Star Princess*) to develop the new Ocean Village brand, designed as an informal expedition for the young adult, the ship herself renamed *Ocean Village* and her hull defaced with the marks of youthful vigour. She also carries her brand name in at least eight locations on the hull and superstructure, the assumption being that the young travellers

The *Oceana* (2000) setting out on a cruise from Southampton in July 2003.

of today need repetitive messages to recognise their own ship come sailing time. There are no set meal times and all meals are informal buffets – perhaps the young cannot yet cope with so many knives and forks. The *Ocean Village* also tends to stay in port for longer periods than the conventional cruise ship so that passengers can sample the local nightlife. In April 2007 she was joined by the *Ocean Village Two*, transferred within the Carnival Group from Aida Cruises where she was formerly the *AIDABlu*. Built as Princess Cruises' *Crown Princess*, she joined the German club-ship scene as the *A'rosa Blu*, and has flown the Red Ensign since May 2000.

The Aida Cruises brand of young adult club ships aimed at the German market now has four ships in service, all of which are registered under Italian ownership. These are the *AIDACara*, *AIDAVita*, *AIDAAura* and *AIDADiva*, with three more ships on order for delivery before 2010.

The year 2005 saw even more change, with the *Adonia* reverting to Princess colours as *Sea Princess* once again, but intended largely for the UK market despite being flagged out of the UK register. The *Sea Princess* displaces the former UK cruise ship the *Royal Princess*, which, after refit to make her more appealing to conservative British tastes, was introduced in the spring of 2005 as P&O Cruises' *Artemis* under a foreign flag. The P&O Cruises brand was boosted again in 2005 by taking delivery of the new *Arcadia*, which was originally laid down as the *Queen Victoria* for Cunard. She was completed as a P&O ship, because it was decided that her main features, including outside veranda cabins and many of her public rooms, were more in keeping with modern-day cruise ships than the traditional liner concept that the *Queen Mary 2* and the Cunard brand purport to be. However, like the *Artemis*, the *Arcadia* is flagged out to the Crown Dependency of Bermuda to attract tax benefits, so the new ship hardly reflects the real image of P&O, whose passenger ships all proudly bore London as their port of registry on the stern. A new liner-styled cruise ship, the *Queen Victoria*, joined the Cunard fleet late in 2007, and the Bermudan-flagged *Ventura* will add to the

The *Ocean Village* (1989) setting out in the rain and dusk on 29 April 2003 on her maiden cruise under the Ocean Village brand, on a positioning run to the Mediterranean from Southampton.

P&O brand in April 2008. The *Ventura* is another of the Grand Princess-class and will be adapted to the British market complete with a Marco Pierre restaurant, 'Cirque Ventura' entertainment troupe, a partnership with the Tate Modern and one with Noddy, the latter presumably for the younger clientele! It is a shame, however, that few of the newer ships that have been designed for the British cruise market can rise to British registration.

Although the three Queens will work together for a short while, the withdrawal and sale of the *Queen Elizabeth 2* has already been arranged with Istithmar, United Arab Emirates, who will give the ship a permanent static role near Dubai from November 2008. The 'QE2' will carry out a final Atlantic tour, leaving Southampton on 10 September for New York and returning via other northern American and Canadian ports at the end of the month. The round trip fare ranges from just over £4,000 to £17,000.

With so much new building and inter-transfer of ships, it is hard for the casual observer to keep abreast of developments. The current boom in worldwide cruising is not expected to wane for some considerable time, and the situation can only become ever more complicated. The Carnival concept revolves firmly around 'big is beautiful'; the economies of scale that size affords and the range of onboard facilities this allows, plus maintenance of interesting itineraries focused on first-class accommodation and the best in entertainment.

A number of UK travel companies own or charter foreign-flagged (crown dependencies and others) ships. These include SAGA, My Travel, Thomson, First Choice, Page & Moy and Voyages of Discovery, the latter company's *Discovery* being none other than the former 'love boat' *Pacific Princess*.

However, despite all this, an opposing view of the market is that 'small is better'. This is only a very tiny niche, but one that is aimed at an elite clientele. One of the smallest of the British

The *Hebridean Princess* (1964) arriving at Oban at the end of a week-long cruise around the Western Isles.

cruise ships in recent years has been the little *Hebridean Princess*. She was initially equipped to transport forty-six passengers in deluxe country house hotel-style accommodation around the Western Isles of Scotland, Scandinavian and Irish Sea destinations, with a crew of just twenty-seven. She had been built in 1964 as a side-loading vehicle and passenger ferry for use by David MacBrayne Limited, and later Caledonian MacBrayne, in which guise she was licensed to carry 600 passengers.

Hebridean Island Cruises Limited started trading in 1988, based at Harrogate. The aim was to offer exclusive 'yacht-style' cruises around the inaccessible, but more attractive, parts of the Western Isles of Scotland. The ferry *Columba*, formerly on the Oban to Mull route, was acquired in 1989. Initially, the vessel retained a car-carrying capability, and the cruises were marketed with the option of joining and leaving at ports of call other than Oban. Within two years the concept had been refined. The car-carrying capacity was removed and additional crew cabins were constructed to allow an increase in the crew-to-guest ratio. By 1997, a crew of thirty-seven was serving just forty-nine passengers.

In 1998 a small company, Hebridean Cruises plc acquired the business. Looking to the future, the 4,200-ton *Megastar Capricorn* was bought from Star Cruises of Malaysia in March 2001 for £11.2 million. A share-issue subscribed mainly by past clients of Hebridean Island Cruises funded the purchase of the ship. The ship was renamed *Hebridean Spirit* and, like the *Hebridean Princess*, registered at Glasgow, and put through a £4.5 million refit at Great Yarmouth. The interior was entirely redesigned to accommodate around eighty guests, while maintaining the same high standards as those of the *Hebridean Princess*. The *Hebridean Spirit* can visit isolated coves and secluded channels inaccessible to larger cruise ships.

The *Hebridean Spirit* (1991) approaching Tower Bridge and the Pool of London stern-first in June 2003.

The ship has been equipped in a discreet but luxurious style with many unusual touches, including a three-ton, bath stone inglenook fireplace, and individually designed and decorated cabins. Following her christening by HRH The Princess Royal on 3 July 2001, *Hebridean Spirit* embarked on her maiden voyage, with international tour programmes to many global destinations. Cruises last between three and seventeen days, and are sold as inclusive fly-cruises, joining and leaving the ship at a variety of different ports. Captain Brian Larcombe commands a crew of around seventy, which includes a tour manager, guide, musician – whose main instrument is obviously the bagpipes – spa therapist and chef de cuisine.

There are forty-nine bedrooms which are named after Scottish islands, castles, clans and glens. Each of the thirty-three double rooms and the sixteen singles provides an elegant surrounding, much in the style of a large private yacht. The two premier suites, the St Columba and St Oran, comprise a large separate dayroom, a spacious bedroom and a luxuriously equipped marble bathroom. The bedrooms are large, and each has a sitting area, some with sofas and most with Italian burr maple furniture. Recreational facilities include a library, a plunge pool on the Mizzen Deck, a beauty spa with treatment room, hair salon, fitness and steam rooms. Evening entertainment features the ship's musician, who is also responsible for piping the departure of the ship from each port.

The chefs devise menus that make extensive use of local produce. There are two weekly black-tie dinners, other nights being less formal. The *Hebridean Spirit* offers single-sitting dining in the elegant Argyll Restaurant. Breakfast and lunch can also be taken outside in the Mizzen Deck Brasserie, weather permitting. Both the *Hebridean Spirit*, on the international cruise venue, and *Hebridean Princess*, on the Scottish and near-field cruises, rely heavily on repeat bookings and are successful in filling an elite and expensive niche market.

Scottish cruises are now also offered by Noble Caledonia using the *Lord of the Glens*. This small vessel was intended for use in Scotland in the summer and the French waterways in the winter. There are just twenty-seven cabins located over three passenger decks. Her summer roster is a thirteen-day cruise between Inverness and Ullapool via the Caledonian Canal, and the islands of Eigg, Rum, Muck and Skye. Although the ship was built in 1985, she was extensively refitted for the service in 2000. She has the distinction of being the only cruise ship ever to be registered at Inverness although, unlike the *Hebridean Princess*, there are few Scots accents to be heard amongst her crew.

FROM CAR FERRY TO *HEBRIDEAN PRINCESS* AND ROYAL YACHT

Who would have guessed, on the retirement of the relief car and passenger ferry *Columba* from Western Isles duties in 1988, that she would still be gainfully employed in these same waters twenty years later? And if, in 1988, you had looked at the old and disused ferry would you have dreamt that she would one day become the Royal Yacht? Nobody had such dreams, as it was obvious the *Columba* would follow her two sisters into service on some workaday chore far from home.

The three car ferries were built by Hall Russell at Aberdeen, the company whose very last order was the *St Helena*, the passenger and cargo liner that now serves St Helena from Cape Town and sometimes the UK. The ferries were built for the Secretary of State for Scotland for operation and management by David MacBrayne Limited, later passing into the ownership of the ferry company Caledonian MacBrayne. The first of the three ferries was the *Hebrides*, taking her maiden voyage from Uig, Skye, on 8 April 1964. She carried the bell of the MacCallum Orme steamer *Hebrides* (see Chapter 1) in her lounge, a reminder of how famous the ship's name was. The ships were side hoist-loading vehicle ferries, there being no linkspans in place back then to serve end-loading ferries. The garage deck headroom was a mere 3 metres so that only cars, light vans and caravans could be carried, or the deck space could be utilised for cattle stalls. The next ship to leave Aberdeen was the *Clansman*, and at the end of July 1964 the third car ferry, the *Columba*, arrived at her new base of Oban.

The new ships had a number of interesting features. One of these was that they were equipped with an external water spray system capable of washing away radioactive fallout. In addition they had a hermetically sealed citadel area that would enable them to carry out a wartime function of hospital ship or command centre. The Cold War, it seems, was very much on the Government's mind at this time. However, the three rather beamy car ferries were found to be difficult to manoeuvre at close quarters to jetties and early opportunity was taken to modify their rudders to overcome this problem. Their accommodation was licensed for 600 passengers in summer, and reduced to 400 in winter. The three revolutionary ferries were an immediate success.

Eventually displaced by second generation end-loading ferries, the *Clansman* was sold in 1984 and the *Hebrides* in 1987. The *Columba* had been acting as the Caledonian MacBrayne reserve vessel for a number of years, but she too was sold in 1988 with her new owners intent on converting the ferry into a Princess. She emerged from her shipyard at Great Yarmouth still very much recognisable as her former self. However internally all had changed. The newly converted cruise ship *Hebridean Princess* now featured a series of themed state rooms with magnificent public rooms and a real stone fireplace emulating the atmosphere of the country house hotel. The stated aim of Hebridean Island Cruises Limited was to share the beauty of the Western Isles from a relaxed but opulent setting. Ownership of the *Hebridean Princess* passed to Hebridean Cruises plc in 1998.

One of the key features of the cruises is the internationally excellent standard of the galley. A small ship capable of entering many of the small harbours in the islands, she tends to cruise from one overnight stop to another allowing passengers time ashore by day, but a silent and peaceful ship either safely tied up or at anchor in some quiet loch by night. Her season lasts from March through to October, allowing an extensive winter lay up period for surveys and maintenance work. Her normal routine is a Thursday evening departure from Oban returning at 7 a.m. the following Thursday. Routine is broken with round-Britain, Irish and other forays during the season.

The *Hebridean Princess* has been a hugely successful venture, providing cruises for an elite clientele with an incredible 60 per cent rebooking record. Now the one-time rust-streaked ferry turned *Hebridean Princess* has received Royal acclaim. Her Majesty Queen Elizabeth II inspected the ship alongside HMS *Belfast* in the Pool of London in September 2005 whilst the *Hebridean Princess* was on normal cruise duties. Subsequently, the *Princess* was adopted as the Royal Yacht for the Queen's eightieth birthday celebrations in the Western Isles in August 2006. Which other cruise ship operator can claim 'by appointment to HM Queen Elizabeth II'?

WHERE TO NEXT?

[I] came on deck at two o'clock in the morning, to see a noble full moon sinking westward, and millions of the most brilliant stars shining overhead. The ship went rolling over a heavy, sweltering, calm sea. The breeze was a warm and soft one; quite different to the rigid air we had left behind us, off the Isle of Wight.

From William Thackeray, Diary of a Voyage from Cornhill to Grand Cairo, 1846.

During a late-night chat show in March 2005 news reporter and television personality John Sargeant described a cruise he had been invited to join as a lecturer. Many of the passengers were very old, he said, so old that few managed to get off the ship at ports of call! One old lady confided in him that she had gone round the world eleven times without ever getting off. Although this could have been a vision of cruising some years ago, it is much less valid now with themed cruises targeted at a variety of age groups.

The appeal of sea travel, excellent hotel service and exotic ports and shore excursions has grown immensely. Although the growth of the cruise industry is now slowing down in the United States, it continues to develop in Europe, not least in the UK. With few exceptions, ships get bigger, and the operators become more global. But where will it all end? The industry still has a few problems to conquer; one of these is shipboard disease, another is rough weather and shallow draft – tall ship design – and a third is mechanical failure, whilst onboard policing is an increasing problem.

Shipboard disease is exemplified by the Pasewalk Virus. In October 2003 the *Aurora* caused an international incident during the course of a Mediterranean cruise. She had suffered a minor and contained outbreak of the Pasewalk Virus earlier in the year, but with 1,800 passengers aboard, at least one of whom had brought the highly contagious flu-like virus aboard at Southampton, the *Aurora* again set off to the sun. By the time she had got to Venice she had 560 sick passengers and crew aboard. Scheduled calls remained at Dubrovnik, Piraeus and Gibraltar. The Greeks refused her permission to dock at Piraeus, but did send vital medical aid and other supplies out to the ship. She finally made landfall at Gibraltar, but half an hour before the *Aurora* docked the Spanish Government closed the border with Gibraltar, opening it only after the ship had sailed for Southampton that evening. The Spanish guards continued to harass people entering Spain for a couple of days by

The *Regal Princess* (1991) arriving at Dublin on 22 August 2003 whilst on a positioning cruise from the Baltic to New York. An army of cleaners met the ship to spend the day cleaning and disinfecting to combat a shipboard outbreak of the Norwalk virus.

insisting on spot-medical-checks, causing long queues and international disquiet. The ship was washed down from top to bottom with disinfectant on her return to the UK.

The disease is surprisingly common among cruise passengers, requiring only one passenger to bring it on board, and it spreads by hand contact rapidly. The *Regal Princess* had completed her summer season in the Baltic in August 2003, and within three days of sailing from Copenhagen had 200 affected passengers en route for New York. On arrival at Dublin, the ship was sprayed and cleaned throughout, although the disease remained virulent aboard ship all the way across the Atlantic.

The *Aurora* is often highlighted on travel programmes as a ship that does not travel well in high seas. Yet the problem is not unique to vessels on which the champagne bottle failed to smash during their naming ceremony. The *Royal Princess* (now *Artemis*) has also had a few celebrated transatlantic voyages with water entering cabins through smashed portholes low in the ship's hull. The combination of tall ship and shallow draft will inevitably cause the ship to be uncomfortable in a long swell, although anti-rolling devices can inhibit lateral movement quite effectively.

The bottle of champagne incident came back to haunt the *Aurora* in January 2005 when propulsion failure caused abandonment of her world cruise. Scheduled to depart on 9 January, she sailed around the Isle of Wight instead. A number of delayed starts and further trials in the Channel led to an anticipated departure of 19 January with some ports left out of the original itinerary to make up time. Meanwhile passengers enjoyed a free bar and excursions out of Southampton to a variety of wintry English destinations. On 20 January the cruise was finally abandoned and passengers were given a full refund. In front of the national press, the ship was humiliated as a laughing stock, whilst the passengers returned home – some content with ten days' free holiday entertainment, others disgusted at their lot. The press, of course, explained that none of the propulsion pod problems would ever have arisen had the champagne bottle broken on the ship's bows in the first place. The cost to Carnival Cruises of a major unit being out of action for three months: £22 million.

The situation was repeated just over a year later when a *Sea Princess* Mediterranean cruise was cancelled at Southampton in May 2007. A spokesman said: 'We are sorry for the upset and inconvenience but we are sure you will understand our need to take the ship out of service so that we can fully complete repairs prior to commencing the European programme as scheduled on 26 May.' Over 2,000 intending passengers were given a full refund plus a 25 per cent credit towards an additional cruise.

Onboard policing is becoming another important issue. There were fourteen passengers reported missing from cruise ships during the years 2004 and 2005, but there is no international tracking of crimes carried out at sea. Theft is apparently on the increase, whilst Carnival reported dealing with 108 complaints of sexual assault between the years 1994 and 1998 (more recent data has not yet been released). The prevailing law on a cruise ship is variable, and may either be the country in whose waters the crime was committed in, or the 'law of the flag' when at sea.

These issues apart, the cruise industry goes from strength to strength. Orders for new and bigger ships continue to be placed, and there seems to be no end to the succession of new and larger tonnage that has characterised the last ten years. Ships will get bigger and talk is now of the 500,000-ton class of vessel. The pleasure of being one passenger amongst a passenger complement of 5,000 is, however, debatable. It will be interesting to see if there will be a swing towards smaller, more elitist vessels for those that can afford to travel in them, leaving the bigger vessels to those of us who are less well-off. After all, as Hebridean Cruises would tell us, smaller ships can enter smaller and potentially more interesting ports; certainly the passengers can be dispatched on shore excursions and fed at mealtimes on a more personal basis than is possible aboard the biggest cruise ships.

That being said, 2006 was another record year for the UK cruise industry. The Passenger Shipping Association reported that 1.2 million British passengers took an ocean cruise, an increase of nearly 12 per cent on the previous year and of 100 per cent on the year 1996. The Caribbean and Alaska were particularly popular among UK travellers. The PSA observed additional growth in niche operators and specialist destinations as UK holidaymakers sought an alternative cruise experience. William Gibbons, director of the PSA, said:

> The strong growth will continue with an estimated 1.3 million British cruise holidaymakers in 2007 and 1.5 million in 2008. The British cruise market also showed the biggest growth rate of all the European countries. In 2008 we will see a very significant increase in growth from the UK, with new ships coming in aimed specifically at the UK market, including *Queen Victoria* (Cunard Line) and *Ventura* (P&O Cruises).

Amazingly, the attraction of the world cruise remains buoyant despite most holidaymakers preferring one-, two- or three-week trips only. However, many passengers now buy segments of the twelve-week cruise, flying out and back to join the ship. The world cruise suffered with the withdrawal of the *Caronia* in 1967, although this role was later picked up by the *Queen Elizabeth 2*, at one stage alternating annually with the French Line's *France*, so that only one ship offered the round-the-world cruise each year.

The *Queen Mary* 2 (2003) makes an impressive sight as she passes Calshot Castle at the start of a cruise on 24 July 2007.

It is worth remembering the annual statement made in 1966 by Sir Basil Smallpiece, chairman of the Cunard Line, the year after his passenger ships had lost £2.7 million:

> If we were to continue to regard our passenger ships only as transport vehicles for carrying people from one place to another, the outlook would be grim indeed. In the field of mere transportation the aeroplanes have captured the market. But if in terms of the marketing concepts we regard the passenger ship no longer simply as a means of transport, but even more a floating resort in which people can take a holiday and enjoy themselves, and incidentally get transportation thrown in, then the market outlook is completely changed. For instead of trading in a contracting market we shall find ourselves in a growth industry, the leisure industry.

The day of the British-registered cruise ship may nearly be over. Whether Carnival's belief that the cost benefits of tax-positive flags outweigh the selling-power of a UK-registered ship with British officers to the British cruise passenger remains to be seen. So here is the conundrum – Britain cannot currently produce enough navigation officers to satisfy demand. The Red Ensign is once again recognised as being synonymous with quality and skill (in, for example, towage and oil rig anchor handling) yet Carnival prefer a West Indian flag at the stern or registration in a crown dependency. The cruise industry might be big business, but the margins are obviously critical to reinvestment and to the shareholders – yet the clients themselves are indifferent to the port of registry and are happy with the cosmopolitan make-up of the crews. Over the last century globalisation has successively overtaken the empire, the nation and now Europe. In a recent survey on the demands of cruise passengers carried out by the Passenger Shipping

The smoking room in the late nineteenth century and, inset, the call for dinner. (From the P&O Pocket Book dated 1888)

Association, 35 per cent of those polled highlighted good food and drink, and only 27 per cent the itinerary – perhaps the ship would be better tied up at Southampton for a fortnight so that the risks from bad weather, onboard disease and policing could all be overcome and the operator save on full costs along the way.

Howarth and Howarth, writing in *The Story of P&O* in 1986, tried to make the link between old and new, a link which is as valid today with the P&O brand of cruise ships as it was then:

> P&O Cruises embodies the most direct line back to those original P&O passengers. There is at first glance scarcely anything comparable between a sooty paddle steamer on a voyage to the Iberian Peninsular with Her Majesty's Mails, and the *Royal Princess* cruising in pristine splendour in Glacier Bay, Alaska – yet in 1836 the first *Iberia* was taking holidaymakers to Madeira, and less than a decade later P&O offered Thackeray his 'delightful Mediterranean cruise'.

The international cruise industry will continue to expand for some time to come. The British market can only cease to expand when the generously-pensioned generations of today are succeeded by future generations that may be less well-endowed in their retirement. In the meantime the overall market is being developed by new products aimed both at families and the younger 'Ocean Village' clientele. Whilst the sight of a cocktail bar may once have shocked those 'that had never seen anything gayer than an aspidistra at the entrance to a dining room', entertainment aboard the modern cruise ship would shock those Victorian senses to the very core!

The newly converted *Ocean Village Two* (1997) seen in Southampton Water is typical of the flair for decorative liveries now being used to appeal to younger clientele.

The *Castalia* (1906), see 'A Reminder for Intending Cruise Guests'.

The days when Britain built prestigious ships to milk the dollar from American cruise passengers are long over. The irony now is that the Americans are reaping the harvest from the British cruise passenger with a handful of ships, while only the smaller vessels are contributing to the UK exchequer. Yet the concept of the sea cruise was, and always will be, a very British institution despite the colour of the flag flying at the stern.

A REMINDER FOR INTENDING CRUISE GUESTS...

The following passage is taken from the wartime diaries of the author's father, George Robins, (diaries which were kept in violation of Naval Regulations) whilst he was deployed as Naval Signalman aboard merchantmen in convoy. The excerpt provides two strong messages: one, that there are two enemies during war, and two, there is still one enemy even in peacetime. It is presented here as a reminder to intending cruise ship guests so that they do not complain when the swimming pool slops over the deck or when a decorative tree is 'dislodged' in the lounge during the night. The ship was the Anchor Line's *Castalia*, built on the Clyde in 1906 with accommodation for just over 100 passengers. She was eventually broken up in 1954, having been sold to Italian owners in 1949. The incident occurred about 70 miles west of Malin Head:

The sea had been rough all day, Sunday 19 October 1941, but it was not until 1530 hours that I began to notice that we were rolling very heavily. About 1500 the wind, which had been blowing strongly for several hours, began to increase very rapidly. By 1600 it had reached Strong Gale force and the Commodore gave the order to the convoy, to 'Heave to'. Already two ships had hoisted 'Not under control' signals. The wind, which was increasing all the time, was whipping the sea into a fury, and by 1700 our ships were spread over a very wide area, the nearest one to us being about five miles away.

At 1800 hours we were struck by a big sea which smashed a number of skylights and portholes, flooding the bar on A Deck and many of the cabins on B Deck. The water, which had no outlet, was rushing up and down the alleyways on B Deck making things very unpleasant.

I was on watch from 1800 to 2000 hours and it was only then that I realised how bad things were. It was easily the worst weather I had experienced. The waves, which we were meeting on the starboard bow, were often towering high above the bridge. The wind was raging through the rigging and made it very difficult at times to get one's breath. The *Castalia* was riding the seas very well but occasionally she nosed down into a big wave in such a way as to make one wonder if she would come right herself again. The violent pitching and rolling of the ship made it essential to hang on to some fixed object all the time, and one had to be ready to duck down behind the dodger at any moment to avoid the full force of waves or heavy loads of spray that often shot over the bridge.

At about 2200 hours the most frightening episode of the night took place. I had been glad to come off watch at 2000, and was at the time in the saloon, when we heard a heavy wave crash on to deck overhead. People who were on the bridge at the time told me that this giant wave crashed down from funnel height. The amidships starboard doors on A and B Decks were stove in, as also was one cabin door on A Deck. The water streamed through the alleyways flooding also all the cabins that were still dry. All gear had to be quickly moved from my cabin, which presented a sorry spectacle. Fortunately all my goods were safe, but the majority of people were less lucky, some cabin-trunks and cases were half-floating half-sliding in the connecting alleyway and I fear the contents must have been ruined. The ship's carpenter and some of the engineers speedily set to work to shore up the smashed outer doors and the stewards got to work baling out as much water as possible from the cabins and alleyways. The main force of this monster wave, however, had struck the after well-deck, where a lifeboat was stove in, three 10ft ventilators were smashed to the deck, and part of the steel railing was buckled as if it had been part of a boy's toy. The officers and crews quarters were in a sorry plight, being well and truly soaked. The most serious damage, though, was the smashing of the steam-pipe, running along this deck, from the engine-room to the steam steering-engine, forcing the ship to be steered by hand from the poop, a job which took the full strength of six men to do.

Shortly after this the engines broke down, and things really looked serious, for now we were drifting helplessly. Several times waves crashed over us, and we wondered if the end had come but the *Castalia* managed each time, with much shuddering to shake the water from her. The hatch-covers were standing up really well to the battering and although we were leaking, the pumps were able to cope easily with the water inside the ship.

By midnight, to everyone's relief, the wind was beginning to die down. Shortly afterwards another great sea smashed in the temporary alleyway door on B Deck flooding us out once more. By this time the starboard ladder from B Deck to the forward well-deck had been carried away, and the ladder from B Deck to A Deck (port side) was loose and quite unsafe.

By 0300 hours the engines were repaired and we were once more able to steer. During the first few hours of Monday the 20th we had some very anxious moments but the wind, which I found afterwards the Captain had entered in the Log as Twelve on the Beaufort Scale and which he considered at its worst was not far short of 120 miles an hour, was going down as quickly as it came up and the sea was rapidly loosing it viciousness. The general opinion was that if the storm had continued another hour or so we should never have seen the dawn. Even as things were we had been very lucky.

By 0400 hours we were out of danger and by 0700 we were able to proceed on our course. The sea was still very rough but by mid-day it had calmed down sufficiently for the steam steering gear to be repaired. Needless to say there was very little sleep to be had during the night. Most of the passengers, officers and convoy signalmen were resting as best they could in the saloon. The Indian night steward, John, and the Scots stewardess, Mrs. Cameron, performed wonders during the night, having a constant supply of tea for tired passengers and almost worn-out engineer and deck officers.

For almost all, if not all of us, this night will set the standard by which all future rough weather will be judged, and I can quite imagine when anyone mentions dirty weather to any of my shipmates of this eventful night the reply will be, 'Rough! You ought to have been in the *Castalia* in '41'.

REFERENCES

Bowen, F.C., *London Ship Types*. The East Ham Echo, London. 1938.

Cartwright, R. and Harvey, C., *Cruise Britannia*. Tempus Publishing Ltd, Stroud. 2004.

Gardiner, R., *The History of the White Star Line*. Ian Allan Publishing Ltd, Hersham. 2001.

Green, E. and Moss M., *A Business of National Importance: The Royal Mail Shipping Group 1902-1937*. Methuen & Company, London. 1982.

Harrower, J., *The Wilson Line: The History and Fleet of Thos. Wilson Son & Co. and Ellerman's Wilson Line*. The World Ship Society, Gravesend. 1998.

Harvey, W.J. and Telford, P.J., *The Clyde Shipping Company*. Glasgow. P.J. Telford. 2002.

Howarth, D. and Howarth, S., *The Story of P&O: The Peninsular & Oriental Steam Navigation Company*. Weidenfeld & Nicolson, London. 1986.

Laird D., *Paddy Henderson: The Story of P. Henderson & Company*. George Outram & Company, Glasgow. 1961.

McRonald, M., *The Irish Boats: Volume 2 – Liverpool to Cork and Waterford*. Tempus Publishing Ltd., Stroud. 2006.

Miller, W., *British Ocean Liners: A Twilight Era, 1960–1985*. Patrick Stephens, Wellingborough. 1986.

Robins, N.S., *The British Excursion Ship*. Brown, Son & Ferguson Ltd, Glasgow. 1998.

Robins, N.S., *The Decline and Revival of the British Passenger Fleet*. Colourpoint Books, Newtownards. 2001.

Robins, N.S. and Meek, D.E., *The Kingdom of MacBrayne*. Birlinn Limited, Edinburgh. 2006.

Vernon Gibbs C.R., *The Western Ocean Passenger Lines and Liners 1934 to 1969*. Brown Son & Ferguson Ltd, Glasgow. 1970.

Watson, M.H., *Disasters at Sea*. Patrick Stephens Limited, Yeovil. 1995.

INDEX OF SHIP NAMES

If you are interested in purchasing any other books published by The History Press, or in case you have difficulty finding any of our books in your local bookshop, you can also place orders directly through our website

www.thehistorypress.co.uk